POLICE SELECTION BOARDS

POLICE SELECTION BOARDS

1ST EDITION

Ian Hutchison

Publisher's Note
Every possible effort has been made to ensure that the information contained in this book is accurate at the time of going to press and the publishers and author cannot accept responsibility for any errors or omissions, however caused. No responsibility for loss or damage occasioned to any person acting, or refraining from action, as a result of the material in this publication can be accepted by the editor, the publisher or the author.

First published in Great Britain in 2009 entitled ***Police Selection Boards***
First edition 2009

Apart from any fair dealing for the purpose of research or private study or criticism or review as permitted under the Copyright, Designs and patents Act 1988, this publication may only be reproduced, stored or transmitted, in any form or by any means, with the prior permission in writing of the publishers, or in the case of reprographic reproduction in accordance with the terms and licences issued by the CLA. Enquiries concerning reproduction outside these terms should be sent to the publishers at the under mentioned address:

ISP Consultancy Ltd
1 Captains Gorse
Upper Basildon
Reading
RG8 8SZ
United Kingdom
www.ispconsultancy.com

© Ian Hutchison, 2009
The right of Ian Hutchison to be identified as the author of this work has been asserted by him in accordance with the Copyright, Designs and Patents Act 1988

British Library Cataloguing in Publication Data

A CIP record for this book is available from the British Library

ISBN 978-0-9554307-1-8

Printed and Bound in Great Britain by Lightning Source, Milton Keynes

For Lorraine, Mollie and Max

Contents

Foreword i
Acknowledgements v

1. **Introduction** 1
2. **Personality** 17
3. **Team working** 49
4. **Leadership** 75
5. **Management** 113
6. **Matching to core competencies** 127
7. **Matching to strategy** 155
8. **Diversity** 175
9. **Interview techniques** 201
10. **Personal action planning** 227

Appendices: 251

National Occupational Standards 253
About ISP Consultancy Ltd. 271

Foreword

Annie Wallis
Nottinghamshire Police

Having personally been through the OSPRE examinations and preparing for the promotion process I am fully aware of the considerable commitment required to pass. But that is only half the story. After celebrating your success there is even more commitment required to successfully negotiate the force selection board.

The selection board is serious business; you will be competing with colleagues for a limited number of vacancies. Make no bones about it there are some really good people out there and the competition will be stiff. You will need to adopt a structured approach to preparing for the board and work really hard if you are to stand a chance of success.

This same principle applies to those of you who are seeking to get on to a specialist department. In some respects the competition is fiercer and you will need to stand out from the crowd if you want to be selected.

By purchasing this book, reading each chapter in detail and making an honest self-assessment of where you are in relation to each topic you will, in my opinion, significantly increase your chances of success. The development plan that follows will focus your mind and energies in the right direction so that you do not waste time on the areas that are perhaps less important.

I have been fortunate enough to meet the author and attended one of his promotion development courses. If you are wondering how I got on; I was successful. I passed my force HPDS board with an A grade and my promotion board with an A grade.

Even if you do not attend one of the courses this book is an excellent start point. My only regret is that by reading this book you will miss the opportunity of meeting Ian himself. Words cannot convey the enthusiasm that he has for developing the careers of those officers he has contact with.

The wide experience he has gained in the armed services and as a police officer has given him a depth and credibility that is captured in this book. He has the ability to instill confidence in people, draw out their strengths and create a 'can do' approach to the selection process. When I first met Ian he had already retired but I was amazed by his energy, drive and passion for policing. He wants the people he comes into contact with to prepare well, believe in their own ability and ultimately pass the selection process.

I have often thought why Ian invests so much time and effort in the careers of others. I realize now that he takes a personal interest in people and still has the passion for policing that he displayed throughout his career. He wants to ensure that police forces across the country recruit good people and then select the right people for specialist departments and promotion. He is also committed to people in the service who aspire to be professional and meet the demands of modern day policing.

If you are one of those people, then use this book to help you progress. It will provide you with a solid foundation that comprises essential information, self assessment, sound advice and a structured approach to your preparation for the selection board process. I would also urge you to read it again after you have been successful at the selection process, because that is just the beginning. What you learn from this book will build the foundations for your career.

I now look to the future with confidence knowing where I am going, what skills I need to develop and how my professional development will be an ongoing process for the remainder of my career.

Acknowledgements

I would like to thank Siri Moorby, my respected colleague, for supporting and encouraging me to write this first edition. I would also like to thank her for carrying out research and for tirelessly proof reading and correcting my terrible grammar.

Chapter 1

Introduction

Aims

If you are reading this introduction I am fairly certain you must be a police officer who is seeking to get promoted, move into a specialist role, get accepted for the High Potential Development Scheme or trying to understand why you have not been successful at a previous police selection board.

Assuming this is the case; I have written this book with your needs in mind and determined that there are some fundamental issues that you need to address. Therefore, I have decided the aim of this book is to:

1. Demystify the police selection board process and enable applicants to understand what is being looked for and why it is done that way.

2. Provide candidates with essential knowledge and understanding of subjects that are fundamental to the board process.

Introduction

3. Provide candidates with a self-assessment tool that helps them discover areas of strength and areas for development.

4. Assist candidates to build development plans that are dynamic, relevant to their work environments and supported by their immediate managers.

Before describing what is in this book and how it works I would like to briefly look at the history of the police selection board, my personal experience as a candidate and as a board member. I will also look at how boards operate and what personal development I experienced during my service

Background

The modern day police selection board has its roots deep in the past and will be found in the origins of the Civil Service Selection Board. The Civil Service Board consisted of a number of different exercises designed to identify relevant skills to do the job and the information gathered from the exercises was used to inform the panel members who conducted the final interview.

The Royal Navy, Army and Royal Air Force have used a version of the civil service model for many years. For example, the Army uses a four day selection process for officer selection at Westbury, Wiltshire, known as the Army Officer

Selection Board (AOSB). This incorporates a number of different exercises that include arithmetic, verbal reasoning, team working, command tasks, briefing and planning. After this, there are a series of interviews. The exercises provide information about the candidate and the interviews probe and fill out what has been collected through the exercises.

The Police

In the police environment we tend to refer to the exercises as the assessment centre and the interview as the selection board. Increasingly, police forces are using a three stage process which incorporates an application, an assessment centre and an interview. For the purposes of simplicity this book will refer to the interview as the board. Although the board is the focus for this book the learning will also aid preparation for the application and the assessment centre.

To a degree, the various stages that police forces build into their selection processes are filters. For example, a competency based application form or a fully evidenced Performance Development Review (PDR) is often used as stage one. The evidence is examined to determine whether an individual is qualified to go forward to the next stage. Those that do may then have to go through an assessment centre designed by the force. After these two stages, in

Introduction

almost all selection processes, there will be a board. The approach does vary from one force to another.

Those fortunate enough to arrive at the door to the selection board will be pleased to be there, but apprehensive. After the board, candidates are often mystified, traumatized and astonished by the iniquity of the whole process.

Candidates who fail to convince the board they should be selected are often heard making comments like, 'What was that all about?'; 'I couldn't work out where it was all going'; 'How can they pass that person with three years service when I have got twenty years in?' Such comments clearly express a degree of frustration with the process.

My experience as a candidate in selection processes is fairly broad. I have appeared before the Regular Commissions Board (now Army Officer Selection Board), the Admiralty Selection Board for the Royal Marines, the Police High Potential Development Scheme and numerous selection processes for specialisation and promotion.

My experience as an assessor and interviewer is also extensive. Having seen it from the other side my perspectives have changed. This transition was not difficult to make as it did not take long to realise just how exposed and under prepared candidates were for the board. For example, as Head of Personnel, I chaired a board for seventy-four candidates seeking promotion to sergeant. This soon became a daily grind searching for sufficient evidence to justify putting candidates through. It was the number of uninspiring performances that created this problem. Occasionally, a candidate would really shine. They were really well prepared and it showed. Sadly, only about five candidates out of the seventy-four fell into this category.

This experience reminded me of a report prepared by my predecessor who had completed a similar marathon. He stated that candidates presenting for promotion were 'uninspiring because they were so poorly prepared.' Precisely my experience.

Why is it that so few candidates are well prepared for the board and success? One reason is the operational imperative. There is always a priority need for vocational skills training, particularly where new and evolving legislation requires it. But even in these cases, police forces still find it difficult to roll out training programmes because of day-to-day operational pressures. There is also constant pressure to develop probationer constables so a lot of energy goes into producing efficient and effective constables. However, beyond this, officers enter a development 'wasteland' where there is no money or time for personal development, even where a process exists. It is hardly surprising that candidates presenting for selection are poorly prepared.

Personal Development

During my service there was no personal development for constables preparing for specialisation. Nor was there any for promotion other than a two week preparation course for the law theory papers that had to be won by competitive examination.

The first time I encountered any true personal development was as a Chief Inspector attending the Junior Command Course at Bramshill. This consisted of a pre-course week with syndicate colleagues where we were put through the Career Development Centre. There were written exercises, letter writing, team working and other exercises that were all assessed. A feedback report was prepared and handed to each candidate at the beginning of the course. This formed the basis of individual personal development plans for the course and beyond.

For me, this was one of the best experiences of my life and I wondered why I had to wait until I became a Chief Inspector to go through this process. I am pretty sure the picture is the same today with operational imperatives a priority and Performance Development Reviews (PDR) taking a back seat.

Introduction

Promotion

You should never make the assumption that because you are good at your present job you are ready for promotion. Being a good constable does not mean that you will be an effective sergeant or that a good sergeant will make an effective inspector. However, it is easy to believe this is the case because the competency based selection process does, to a certain extent, imply this.

Most police forces use a stage one application form, or Performance Development Review (PDR), that asks you to produce evidence of performance in competency areas by describing things you have done in the past. In addition, most police forces have a stage two competency based promotion selection board, usually consisting of two or three panel members. The panel members fire questions at you based on the competencies to tease out whether you match up to the skills required for the next rank.

Confusion arises in the dichotomy between providing evidence of things you have done in the past and convincing them you have the skills to be promoted to the next rank. If you have never been a sergeant how can you provide evidence that you have the skills to do the job? This is even more confusing where an officer has been acting in a rank and still cannot get through a promotion selection board. How often

Introduction

have you heard, "I have been acting sergeant for three years and they still will not put me through a board!"

The basis of competency assessment suggests if you have done something in the past you are likely to do it again in the future. There is some truth in the contention that the past is a predictor of the future, but caution should be exercised when it comes to promotion. The best we get from the past is painting a picture of you as an individual. But the key message here is that the skills required in your current job are not the same as the skills required in the next rank.

Many forces are now looking for you to present evidence from the past that demonstrates you have the skills for the target rank. This means that you will have to evidence the competencies they will be testing you against rather than those of your present rank. This makes things doubly difficult for candidates. However, if you follow the approach to personal development described in this book you will begin to live in the future and these things will become second nature.

Even if you are well prepared for a selection board and you feel you put up a good performance, you may still fail. The reason for this is often more complex than you realise. Police forces have to succession plan and identify people with the right skills to maintain the overall resilience of the force. Promotions, transfers, sickness and retirement are all factors that human resources have to take into account in determining how many and who they will promote. Never make the assumption that it is a level playing field and because you have a good performance on the board you will get through. The survival of the organisation is paramount.

Take, for instance, a substantial loss of experience to the Criminal Investigation Department (CID) through retirement or promotion of senior investigating officers (SIO) in three years time. There is no point in waiting for it to happen because the result would be a skills deficit in crime investigation. Clearly, if those posts need filling it is likely that the careers of detectives need to be managed and they must be promoted to ensure there are sufficient qualified people to compete for the SIO role in three years time. So, this year might be the year of the CID. This principle equally applies to other specialist roles like computers, command and control and preparing for the Olympics, where fast tracking of certain individuals is required.

Nothing in this approach detracts from your own skills and worth to the organisation. It just means that sometimes your progression may appear slower than someone else. If you happen

Introduction

to be in the category they are looking for it may be even quicker than you expected.

Either way, it is important that you have an open mind about your career and you seek feed back on your performance and try to understand the force priorities. In the general scheme of things, if you are good enough, your time will come and it is always useful to look at the career paths of other officers. Some may have spent fifteen years as a sergeant and then been promoted to superintendent in four years. Alternatively, another may be rapidly promoted to inspector and then marked time at that rank for several years before moving on.

One way of dealing with short term disappointments is to ensure you have a good coach and mentor. They will help you to network and understand what is happening in your force.

This Book

One of the key aims of this book is to provide candidates seeking selection with essential knowledge and understanding of subjects that are fundamental to the board process. The list of topics, as you can imagine, is not exhaustive but those contained within the chapters of this book are considered essential and therefore foundations on which other knowledge can be built. The topics are:

(a) Personality

This chapter introduces the fundamental elements of personal development. It defines personality, how to develop it through a self-discovery process and putting together a development plan.

(b) Team Working

This chapter will look at the theoretical aspects of team working by looking at different team roles, team problem solving, team styles and assessing your personal team style.

(c) Leadership

This chapter will discuss leadership theories, leadership styles and assess your personal style. Transformational leadership is an extremely topical subject in police forces across the country as they try to develop a leadership culture in all police and police staff to help create progressive organisations. It is essential that you understand what it is and how it can be distinguished from transactional leadership and the other styles described. It is outlined here to give you a start point for your thinking.

(d) Management

Managing people is fundamental to getting the job done and the focus of situational leadership.

Introduction

This chapter will introduce the five key skills of management and describe the role of the manager as the link between the organisation and the team. It also provides a framework on which to build the theory of the previous three chapters.

(e) Matching to Competencies

Understanding the importance of the core competencies and how they operate is essential. This chapter deals with matching individual skills to the competencies and demonstrates how to use the STAR methodology.

(f) Matching to Strategy

This chapter describes strategy and recognises the relationship between situational vision and leadership. As with matching to competencies, this chapter explains how to match to strategy. There is a focus on Strategic Perspective

(g) Diversity

This is always a topical subject for boards and is sometimes the subject that a whole board can hang on. In this chapter there is a review of the key issues and the requirements of the National Learning Requirement for the police service. This is followed by a review of discrimination law and the National Occupational Standards.

(h) Interview Technique

Technique is just as important as information when it comes to a good performance on a board. In this chapter you will learn what good technique is, how to set the agenda for the interview and how to use a structured approach to answering questions. In addition, you will learn that behaviours like posture and using hands are important.

(i) Personal Action Planning

In this final chapter you will be able to review the personal assessments you have made in the previous chapters. Each mark will be plotted graphically on a 'Spider Chart' to give you a visual representation of your development needs. As a result, you will be able to complete a plan that contains activities to address your development. There is also a section on SMART objectives to help you prepare development objectives. Coaching and mentoring is important to the success of your development plan; a section helps you to identify these people and what you can expect from them. Finally, there is an explanation of experiential learning.

Book Structure and Self Assessment

Each chapter stands alone to enable the reader to dip into topics as they wish, depending on individual needs. However, each chapter should be seen as source of knowledge and an opportunity for self-assessment. At the end of Chapters 2-9 there is a self-assessment page. This is included so that you can assess your current knowledge of the subject and identify what you can do to improve it. You will also be able to make an assessment of your skills and award yourself a mark out of 10.

After awarding marks out of ten for each one they should be transferred into the spider chart in Chapter 10. This will provide a visual representation of your strengths and areas for development. There is nothing scientific about the Spider Chart, it is provided solely for your benefit and, providing you are honest about your knowledge and skills in each area, it will help focus your mind on areas that need developing. A little clarity is often useful in helping you to plan. There is an Activity Chart that you can use to identify key areas of activity for your development plan.

Chapter 10 deals with the whole Personal Action Planning process and also describes how to prepare SMART objectives and get the assistance of a coach and mentor to help you with your development.

Summary

This book will demystify the selection board process and provide essential knowledge for candidates seeking promotion, specialisation or aspiring to be selected for the High Potential Development Scheme. Be bold in gaining the required knowledge and build on it. Remember that this book is just the starting point for the work you need to do to be successful. Also, be bold about your current level of skills and be prepared to assess yourself honestly. Finally, make sure that you follow through with your development plan and get real results. Preparation is the key to success. I wish you success with the board, whatever you aspire to achieve.

Ian Hutchison
February 2009

Chapter 2

Personality

Aims

This chapter will introduce you to the fundamental elements of personality and enable you to:

- **Define personality**

- **Describe personal development**

- **Describe self-discovery**

- **Describe development plans**

- **Assess your current personal development needs**

Introduction

Before looking at the mechanisms we can employ to be successful at a formal interview it is essential to know what we are trying to achieve. Of course, we want to pass the selection board, but do we understand what the interviewers will be looking for during the interview? We must assume they are looking to see if you have the qualities required to do the job. That is simple; but what are the qualities and how do you demonstrate them?

Clearly, the skills required to do the job will be defined by core competencies that are considered essential for the role. The issue is how to demonstrate them effectively. In a written application we can demonstrate them through the completion of competency based answers that provide examples of behaviours we have demonstrated in the past. This paper based process is sufficient to short-list people who appear to have the right experiences and ability to do the job, but the formal interview is the time and place where these attributes will be tested. So, how do you demonstrate that you have the necessary skills in a formal interview?

The answer is simple. We use our **personality** to persuade the panel that we meet the criteria they have set for the job.

You are probably thinking that personality is not a sufficiently robust tool to use in convincing them. Generally, we consider personality to be the type of person we are. We tend to categorise people; some are quiet and others noisy. Some extrovert and others introvert. In reality, however, this is far too simplistic. We are all very complex and unique individuals who possess many attributes. Often, the first impression we have of a person tells us little about the real skills and abilities they possess. First impressions, although important, are short lived.

By way of illustration, a motor car parked in a car park might be eye catching and considered to be a fine example of advanced engineering, with great lines and state of the art specification. But parked in a car park with the engine turned off it does not provide any information about how it drives. Looking good is not always a good testimony to performance.

The lesson to be learned here is that we should not make a quick assessment of a person based on first impressions. We should not make assumptions based on their sex, dress, body shape or demeanor and look deeper to see what is behind the first impressions. Also, we must be aware that what is on the inside must come out and become evident to those who are assessing our skills and abilities for a particular job. So, when you enter the interview room the first impression, albeit important, will only last as long as you can convince the panel you are the person for the job.

What is personality?

The word personality is derived from the Latin word persona that was originally used to denote the different role masks used by actors in Greek plays. Over time the word came to mean the character being portrayed rather than the mask. The origins of the word are not so far from what some psychologists believe about personality today; it is a series of assumed roles we act out in different situations.

Everyday we find ourselves describing and assessing the personalities of those around us. Whether we realise it or not, this is similar to how personality psychologists make assessments. While our informal assessments of personality tend to focus more on individuals, personality psychologists use broad personality styles that can be applied to different people. This has led to the development of a number of theories that help explain how and why certain personality traits develop.

Of course, this view raises the question of whether it is possible to measure a personality that is constantly changing in response to different situations. However, despite adapting our behaviour, we can see a consistency of behaviours across a range of situations and over time.

A simple definition of personality is, *'a person's typical or preferred way of behaving, thinking and feeling'.*

This recognises that while personality is affected by current circumstances and environment, it is possible to identify enduring and stable characteristics. What creates those enduring characteristics is up for debate but it is clear that there is some clarity about factors that influence human personality. For example, age, genetics, family, education, life experience, environment and socio-cultural factors are all important in shaping a personality.

Components of Personality

Although there is constant debate about the construction of personality, psychologists tend to agree on some of the fundamental identifiable characteristics of personality. These include:

(a) Organisation and consistency

In this component different parts of our personality are often linked together and they guide our behaviour in an organised, structured and consistent way.

(b) Psychological and physiological

It is recognised that personality is of a psychological construction, but it is also influenced by physiological processes and needs.

(c) Behavioural

Personality not only influences how we react to our environment, it also influences how we behave in certain situations. Our personalities are demonstrated in many ways through our behaviour, thoughts, feelings and interactions with others.

How does personality develop?

There are a number of theories about the development of personality. Psychologists differ on what impacts on the development of personality, but there are some recognisable major influences. Three of these include:

(a) Behavioural

This suggests that personality is a result of interaction between the individual and the environment. Behavioural theorists study observable and measurable behaviours without taking into account internal thoughts and feelings. Behavioural theorists include B. F. Skinner and John Watson.

(b) Psychodynamic

Psychodynamic theories suggest that personality development is influenced by the unconscious. These theories are heavily influenced by the work of Sigmund Freud.

(c) Humanist

Humanist theories emphasise the importance of free will and individual experience in the development of personality. Humanist theorists include Carl Rogers and Abraham Maslow.

What influences the development of personality?

If we take time out to look around us and assess what is going on in society it is certain we will see that there is much happening. If you use the strategic planner's tool, PESTELO, to analyse the Political, Economic, Social, Technical, Environmental, Legal and Organisational developments in our society we will be amazed at what is going on around us. If we try to project where we will be in ten years from now, it is unlikely that we will be able to accurately predict what will impact on our lives.

Just consider how things have changed in the recent past with Bluetooth, satellite navigation, IPOD, I Phone and other technological advances. Look at the police environment and consider just how much change there has been over the last five or ten years. The speed of change leaves us vulnerable to being left behind. Take for example the National Intelligence Model and how its philosophy directs our thinking.

From the time we are born we grow physically, mentally and emotionally, becoming unique individuals plotting our way through life to become successful and comfortable. Many of the skills we acquire in early life are designed to enable us to deal with the many difficulties we will encounter and help us solve problems as we progress. The key to a trauma free life is 'awareness'. We know what to expect <u>and</u> we know how to deal with it.

With this in mind, it would be very easy to make broad assumptions about the pace and extent of personality development. If we take a look at how William Shakespeare saw our lives it was clear he saw it mapped out in a fairly pre-determined way:

All the world's a stage, And all the men and women merely players: They have their exits and their entrances; And one man in his time plays many parts, His acts being seven ages.

- *At first the infant, Mewling and puking in the nurse's arms.*

Personality

- *And then the whining school-boy, with his satchel And shining morning face, creeping like snail Unwillingly to school.*
- *And then the lover, Sighing like furnace, with a woeful ballad Made to his mistress' eyebrow.*
- *Then a soldier, Full of strange oaths and bearded like the pard, Jealous in honour, sudden and quick in quarrel, Seeking the bubble reputation Even in the cannon's mouth.*
- *And then the justice, In fair round belly with good capon lined, With eyes severe and beard of formal cut, Full of wise saws and modern instances; And so he plays his part.*
- *The sixth age shifts Into the lean and slipper'd pantaloon, With spectacles on nose and pouch on side, His youthful hose, well saved, a world too wide For his shrunk shank; and his big manly voice, Turning again toward childish treble, pipes And whistles in his sound.*
- *Last scene of all, That ends this strange eventful history, Is second childishness and mere oblivion, Sans teeth, sans eyes, sans taste, sans everything.*

All the world's a stage (*from* As You Like It 2/7)

We can all recognise the different phases of our lives that Shakespeare describes. However, the seven ages of man is rather too simplistic. If we accept these milestones and adjust our personalities to deal with each phase, there is a danger we accept life is predetermined. This can lead us to believe that we only need to meet the criteria required to get through each phase. For example, retirement is seen by many people as the time to slow down and do less.

If we believe this we will only develop to meet the challenges of that phase. Our threshold of awareness and skills will be limited to deal with things that challenge us in that phase.

This is the comfort zone where we are comfortable and happy. We cope rather than progress. The longer this state exists the less aware we become and less prepared to deal with life's problems. A good example of this is evident in the so-called generation gap. Younger people are very aware and able to deal with life at the cutting edge and some of us, not so young, do not keep up and fail to understand new approaches and methods. I am sure we have all experienced a moment when a young child has taught an adult how to operate a computer far beyond the level of their comprehension. We have also all met an older retired colleague who has been very complimentary, "I couldn't live with the current pace of policing, we had more time to think and plan in my day."

This is a lack of personal development. The ability to continue solving problems in life and moving forward as opposed to entering the stagnation zone is essential in all phases of our lives. A Chinese proverb sums this up:

"Don't be afraid of going slowly – be afraid of standing still".

In recognising that this state of affairs can exist and affect us, it is useful to define personal development.

Defining Personal Development

Personal development is the gradual process of expanding awareness and consciousness of life. It is also extending capabilities and potential to deal with future challenges.

It is being aware of our feelings, attitudes, behaviours and those of others through being proactive in overcoming faults, weaknesses and insecurities.

Why Develop?

You might ask, 'why develop?' You have passed all your examinations and the future is looking rosy. However, if you are ambitious and keen to climb the ladder, you will inevitably reach a point where your career begins to falter; no matter what you do there seem to be blockages in your way. This will lead to frustration and is demotivating. You may even despair that your career is in tatters, particularly when you see people who are apparently of lesser intellectual ability or experience overtaking and accelerating away from you. Now ask yourself, 'why?' It is no good complaining their success is all down to nepotism because such negativity will prevent you from moving forward. You have to ask why these people have been successful.

Look at your own experience. We all know of those colleagues at school who were exceptionally academically gifted, with high Intelligence Quotient (IQ) and who had little difficulty with their studies. They always excelled in their examinations and probably went on to graduate from university. But where are they now and have they been more successful than the rest of us?

Research evidence suggests that people with the highest IQ scores and exceptional academic ability are unlikely to be more successful, when comparing salaries or status, with colleagues who were not outstanding academics. There is also evidence to suggest that these people do not experience the greatest satisfaction from life or in their personal relationships.

It appears that those of us that do not share outstanding academic ability have much more at stake. Those people who work hard at their personal awareness and extend their capabilities to deal with future challenges will be successful. This also tells us that personal development is not something you can necessarily gain from formal education through the process of gathering knowledge. It is about the maturing and development of the mind to prepare for future challenges.

We are not taught personal development nor are we taught how important it is to understand ourselves. Discovering our personal identity, values, beliefs and attitudes is equally important as cognitive learning. We also need to understand how our personality impacts on others. How we engage with people when first meeting, being positive, showing enthusiasm, controlling temper, using positive non-verbal communication and showing empathy. We all recognise a good boss and people we enjoy being with. Why is that? Ask yourself why an academically unqualified second hand car sales person lives in a big house and drives an expensive car? These are people who understand themselves and are socially confident.

Personal success begins with the development of self-awareness that will enable a positive self-management strategy. After that you will need to develop awareness of the challenges ahead and structure your actions accordingly. Another proverb sums this up:

"Learning to learn is the biggest learning of all"

Discovering Yourself

Discovering yourself is the first step in the process of personal development. It needs to be structured and focused on the purpose of the development. In this case we are looking at key elements of leadership and management in a police environment. Once the process of discovery is complete then a personality profile will have been built and we can begin to prepare a development plan to enhance strengths and develop areas of potential weakness. Depending on the level of self-awareness, a development plan will be pursued over a defined period of time. It is important that the period of development is properly managed around a plan that includes discovery, input and reflection.

Before looking at the process of discovery it is important to understand what makes *you* who *you are*. Your personality is a combination of recognisable characteristics. It is made up of many components all of which you will need to discover. If others can recognise your personality it is extremely important that you recognise and understand it as well.

The Process of Self Discovery

This process is about using simple techniques to tease out the components of your personality. It is possible to break a personality down into as many dimensions (or slices) as you wish. But the more you use the more complex interpretation will become; it is important, therefore, to keep this as simple as possible.

There are a number of different methods of obtaining the information to discover personality.

(a) Psychometric Testing

Using a psychometric instrument is always a useful method of discovering things about personality. Providing it is objectively administered, the subject is honest and open, and the results are fed back to the subject in a constructive way, it will be a positive experience.

Many of these tests are focused on different personality traits and therefore it may be necessary to undergo a number of different tests to discover the various aspects of personality. A better practical approach is to use a test that is comprehensive and, after only one test, many different aspects of personality can be draw from it. The Saville and Holdsworth Occupational Personality Questionnaire (OPQ) is an example of a test that can provide a broad range of information.

The OPQ breaks down personality into 32 dimensions. It provides a picture of personality, team working, leadership, reporting style, emotional intelligence, learning style, management competency and provides a range of development tools.

There are also many other instruments on the market. Some of these can be completed on-line and provide feed back. One of these is Watson Glaser (UK) which is used by the High Potential Development Scheme:
http://www.getfeedback.net/products/detail/ranra.

Whatever testing is used there may be a natural tendency toward cynicism about psychometrics and their accuracy. Accepting that our personalities are not an exact science, we should look on testing as just another tool to help us discover our personality profile. Experience shows that combining psychometrics with the other methods is a complimentary process.

(b) 360 Degree Appraisal

If there is any cynicism about psychometrics then the 360 degree appraisal is the ideal method of balancing perspectives. In this case a questionnaire structured around aspects of personality is issued to a number of work colleagues who are subordinate, contemporary and senior to the subject. The questionnaire is completed by the colleague who will indicate against each of the dimensions whether it is a positive, satisfactory or an area for development. This is completed anonymously and returned to a moderator who will prepare a composite of the results.

This is a picture of how an individual is seen in the real world by a number of different people. If one person was to indicate that you do not listen when people are speaking to you, it is just possible that is indicative of a single bad experience. But, if all of the respondents indicate that you do not listen, then it is time to start listening.

This is a powerful tool and it is about how people see and experience you in the work place. You will soon begin to see a different person in the mirror each morning after going through this process. Subjects are often initially apprehensive about the process but find it rewarding and it can be a key aid in the development process.

(c) Performance Development Review

Annual Performance Development Review (PDR) is an ideal tool to use to identify personality traits and professional skills. The PDR already has a professional section where performance is assessed against annual objectives. Although the evidence is provided by the appraisee for validation by the appraiser the process is largely one dimensional in that there is still an element of top down perspective. Despite this the process is extremely useful in identifying personality.

(d) Work and Life Experiences

Throughout our lives we are constantly subject to experiences that challenge us and test the extent of our ability to deal with them. Sometimes these experiences are ideal examples of when we had to show leadership in a difficult situation or work in a team to get a job done within a very tight time frame. These work and life experiences make up the rich picture of who we are and build the personality that we have. So, it is always a good idea to review these experiences and see what key personality traits came into play at that time.

(e) Special Experiences

These are the experiences we perhaps do not really want to have as part of our lives. You may have been involved in a traumatic incident like a car accident, a train crash, or maybe you have had cancer or experienced the loss of someone close to you through a long and protracted illness.

For most of us these are the type of experiences that have a major impact on how we see the world. Sometimes these life changing experiences have a profound effect on how people lead their lives. It is possible something like this has touched you. Take some time to see how an incident of this kind may have impacted your personality and how your particular traits may have changed as a result.

Summary

These are just some of the methods of gathering information about your personality. The list is not exhaustive and you should be as inventive as possible in discovering yourself.

Areas for Discovery

Now that you have identified how to gather information about yourself, what kind of information do you need to know in relation to selection in the police service? What follows are summaries of areas you should be familiar with.

1. Team Role

It is essential that you understand the work of Dr. R. Meredith Belbin who published 'Management Teams - why they succeed or fail' in 1981. Driven by the increasing importance of team working in organisations at the time, Belbin set out to identify what made a good team, based on research in the UK and Australia. Although the book offered a number of important factors about team working, it is the team roles that became famous.

Belbin found that in successful teams eight roles could be seen in operation and concluded that, when selecting people for a team, filling the eight roles was as important as choosing technical skills or experiences. Belbin's ideas continue to be used by thousands of organisations because they make good sense and they work.

Today there are many different tools to identify individuals' preferred roles, and help teams to make the best use of each role. Although your preferred roles are relatively unchanging over time, most of us can happily perform two or three of the roles, thus filling any gaps in the team's profile. That also means that one person can cover more than one role - clearly important if you have a team of less than eight people!

The concept works best when used openly within a team or across an organisation. Individual preferences are only useful if they are known to others, so teams can assess who can best fulfill each role. You can use role identification as a form of team-building; it reinforces the fact that everyone is bringing something to the team, so you all need each other if you are to be successful.

It follows, that awareness of our own preferred team role and others is a major contributor to understanding personal effectiveness in the work place, ensuring group cohesion and increasing overall organisational achievement. This is an essential skill for all leaders and managers.

2. Leadership Style

Whether you are managing a team at work, the captain of your sports team or leading a major corporation, your leadership style is crucial to your success. Consciously, or subconsciously, you will no doubt use some of the leadership styles featured in Chapter 4, at least some of the time. Understanding these leadership styles and their impact can help you develop and adapt your own leadership style and so help you become a more effective leader.

A good leader will switch instinctively between styles according to the people and work they are dealing with. This is often referred to as situational leadership. For example, the manager of a small factory trains new machine operatives using a bureaucratic style to ensure they know the procedures that achieve the right standards of product quality and workplace safety. The same manager may adopt a more participative style of leadership when working on production line improvement with his or her team of supervisors.

Leadership comes in many guises and is a hotly debated subject. What constitutes this, sometimes elusive, commodity is often defined in different ways. For the sake of argument and simplicity the key principle of leadership is a clear vision of where you are going, the ability to communicate it and take people with you. The Leadership Trust describes leadership as:

"Leadership is using your personal power to win the hearts and minds of people to achieve a common purpose"

How you lead people to your vision is about personal style.

3. Reporting Style

This is about how we respond to and work for our managers. Different personalities prefer to respond to their manager in diverse ways. Some enjoy complete freedom to work autonomously without direct supervision and like to use their initiative to make decisions. At the other end of the spectrum, others may prefer to have opportunities to inject ideas into decision-making but are likely to accept decisions that go against their views.

It is possible to see links with leadership styles in that a self reliant report is more likely to be a directive leader.

4. Emotional Intelligence

Historically, innate intellectual ability was measured through an Intelligence Quotient (IQ). This measure of cognitive capacity typically uncovered intellectual agility in dealing with core academic subjects. Often IQ was used as a predictor of the level of expected academic achievement. It was also accepted that a high or low IQ was said to determine how successful you were likely to be in your working life.

Modern research evidence has questioned how accurate IQ is as a predictor of life success and modern neuroscience has suggested there is much more to it than intelligence levels. The cerebral cortex, the cognitive or thinking part of the brain, cannot work in isolation it requires the sub cortex, the emotional centre of the brain, to work with it. In effect, intellect and emotion are not mutually exclusive. They work together in a complimentary way to determine daily decision-making.

Emotional Intelligence (EI) is best described as: *"a type of social intelligence that involves the ability to monitor one's own and others' emotions, to discriminate among them, and to use the information to guide one's thinking and actions"* (Mayer & Salovey 1995).

Simply put, one needs to be intellectually and emotionally aware to be successful in life. An imbalance or a lack of awareness is a waste of talent. It pays to know both your Intelligence (IQ) and Emotional Quotient (EQ), and get them to work together for you.

To assist in defining and understanding your EQ it is broken down principally into two dimensions.

Managing Feelings is how well you *manage* and *understand* your emotions and feelings.

Managing Relationships is about how well you *appreciate* the perspectives of others and how *flexible* is your style in adapting to different work and social situations.

The importance of EQ insight comes alive when the impact of emotional intelligence is applied to develop other skills like leadership, team working, individual performance, interpersonal exchanges, managing change, and performance assessments. For example, good leadership requires excellent self-awareness, self-control, awareness of others, and social skills. Developing these EQ competences can have a major impact on personal effectiveness.

5. Learning Style

Cognitive learning is an individual experience. We all have a preferred style and it is well known that if a group of people are given the same activity, some learn a lot whilst others learn very little. This is because the activity will not suit all learning styles of those within the group.

It is possible, with reasonable accuracy, to predict individual learning styles through psychometric screening to assist individuals understand and develop the most productive cognitive experiences. Styles fall into four common definitions.

Activist learns best from experiences which are new, competitive, exciting and high profile. They are people that thrive on learning on the job and are not deterred by giving them a high profile.

Reflectors are people that enjoy learning from opportunities where they are able to stand back from events, watch, assimilate and think about what they are seeing before acting.

Theorist likes to have a model, system or theory into which they can link new concepts. A sense of order is preferred to probe basic concepts and assumptions.

Pragmatist learns best from activities that can be linked to the solving of problems or a real life opportunity in their job. Turning the subject matter into a practical reality helps them to learn more easily.

It is important for those who teach us to recognise the need for diverse learning opportunities to reach out and meet student needs. More importantly, in terms of personal development, it is imperative that we understand how, as individuals, we learn best. Without understanding our own preferred style we will not realise or maximise our true potential through the most appropriate and productive learning experiences.

6. Greatest Strength and Weakness

Strength – Make sure that you understand what particular aspect of your personality is your greatest strength. If you know what it is then you can use this as a base line from which you can support the development of other aspects of your personality and maximise your success.

Weakness – We all have development areas that can weaken our performance. Recognising these is important. It does not matter what it is, providing you know how to manage it and turn it into a positive strength.

Often a great strength and a weakness can be the two sides of the same coin. For example, your great strength might be your strong vision and determination to achieve. This is very positive. But your strength will become a weakness if you are so enthusiastic that your drive and determination, particularly where your efforts are frustrated in any way, spill over into arrogance.

Similarly, if you have bags of determination and drive but you fail to communicate your vision to your team and they do not understand what is required, your natural great strength, by default, will become your worst weakness.

An easy way in which to determine your strengths and weaknesses is through a 360 degree appraisal. Always be self-aware in these areas because you can frustrate many of your efforts to be successful purely through having a blind spot. It is so important to your success that you are sensitised to your impact on other people.

7. Career Achievements

As a final step in the process of preparing a personal profile and a development plan, it is essential to assess what you have achieved in your career so far. What you have achieved is key to a synthesis of all the information gathered through the programme of discovery.
A good way of doing this is to gather information under four heads. Identifying the **skills** that you have developed during your working life helps to identify what you can do and what you are best at. Recognising your **attitudes** to life, your work and the future will help to understand the

cultural development you have gone through during your working life. This is useful in modelling styles for your future development plan. Defining the **knowledge** that you have accrued through experiences to date helps in understanding whether you have a technical, strategic, commercial or other area of particular strength. Underpinning these three broad areas is **experience**. Whatever your technical level of skills might be, without exposure to life and work experiences the natural process of continuous learning will not take place. The old adage that there is 'no substitute for experience' and 'you can't put an old head on young shoulders', has some truth. The secret is a subtle blend of all four of these areas.

Personality Profile

After having been through the process of discovery you should have a rich picture of your personality. It is highly likely that you will have uncovered a vast range of skills, many of which are positive strengths and some where development will be of benefit. Either way, you will have a much better appreciation of who you are and you should be able to pull together all the various facets to build a personality profile.

The personality profile will represent a box of jigsaw pieces that need to be sorted and grouped into areas where there are linkages. You will need to build these packages of skills

Personality

into a cohesive framework that you can personally articulate. Consider for one moment if you were asked the question, *'Tell me a little about yourself?'* would you be able to answer that question in a cogent and well structured way? That is your objective in unravelling all of the information you have gathered about yourself.

Personal Action Planning

After sorting the information into a structure that can be articulated you should identify the strengths and weaknesses. Both areas should be subject to a development plan that will reinforce strengths and improve weaknesses. This follows the same planning approach that is fundamental to the Performance Development Review. Each area should be subject to a SMART structured approach.

Specific-Measurable-Achievable-Realistic-Timed

Once this is done, it is a matter of including all the development that is necessary to improve the overall skills package that will make up your personality. The cycle is complete and this becomes a process of continuous professional development (CPD).

Chapter 10, Personal Action Planning, provides detailed information on the development process.

Personality

Process of Discovery and Development

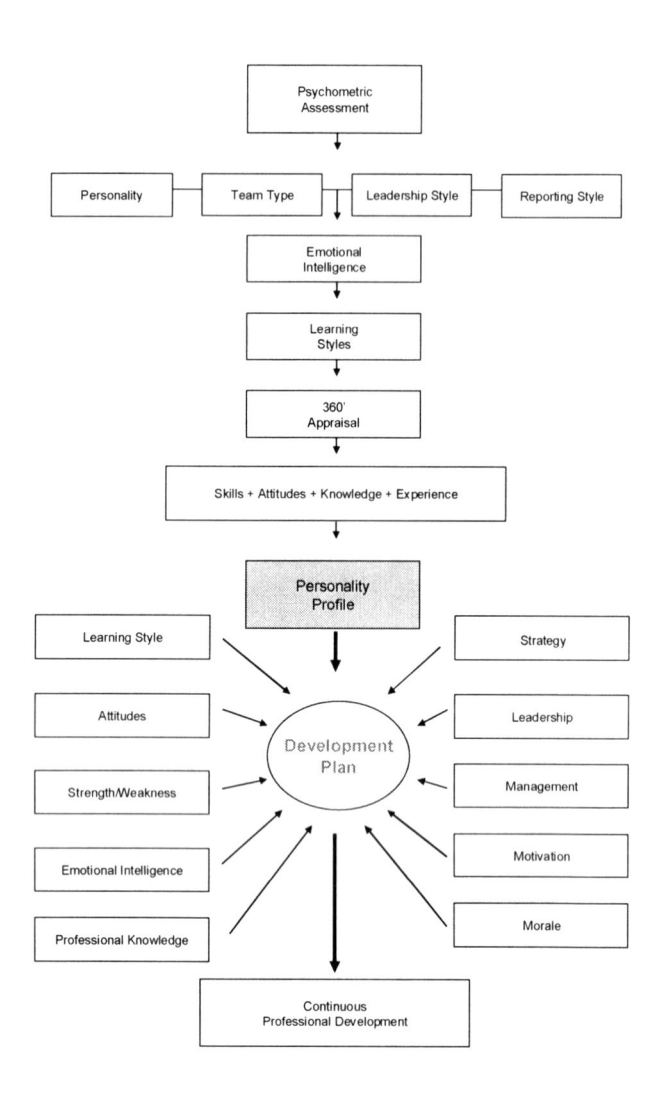

```
                    ┌──────────────┐
                    │ Psychometric │
                    │  Assessment  │
                    └──────┬───────┘
                           ▼
┌───────────┐  ┌───────────┐  ┌────────────────┐  ┌────────────────┐
│Personality│──│ Team Type │──│Leadership Style│──│ Reporting Style│
└───────────┘  └───────────┘  └────────────────┘  └────────────────┘
                           │
                           ▼
                    ┌──────────────┐
                    │   Emotional  │
                    │ Intelligence │
                    └──────┬───────┘
                           ▼
                    ┌──────────────┐
                    │   Learning   │
                    │    Styles    │
                    └──────┬───────┘
                           ▼
                    ┌──────────────┐
                    │     360'     │
                    │   Appraisal  │
                    └──────┬───────┘
                           ▼
        ┌──────────────────────────────────────┐
        │ Skills + Attitudes + Knowledge + Experience │
        └──────────────────┬───────────────────┘
                           ▼
                    ┌──────────────┐
                    │  Personality │
                    │    Profile   │
                    └──────────────┘
```

- Learning Style
- Attitudes
- Strength/Weakness
- Emotional Intelligence
- Professional Knowledge

→ Development Plan ←

- Strategy
- Leadership
- Management
- Motivation
- Morale

↓

Continuous Professional Development

Personality

Personal Development Assessment

Consider what you have learned in this chapter about personality and make an assessment of your developmental needs. This will help you to identify and collate, chapter by chapter, areas you need to consider for inclusion in your Personal Action Plan.

1. What **gaps** in your knowledge do you have on personality?

2. What **actions** can you take in the work place or elsewhere to improve knowledge of your personality?

3. How do you rate your **skills** in this area?

Rate yourself with a score out of 10. (10 high, 1 low)

10

Chapter 3

Team Working

Aims

This chapter will introduce you to the fundamental elements of team working and enable you to:

- **Describe team working**

- **Describe team roles**

- **Describe team problem solving**

- **Describe different team styles**

- **Describe your own team style**

- **Assess your current team working development needs**

Introduction

Team working is present in our personal and professional lives whether as a member of a sports team, voluntary organisation or in the work place solving problems. The importance of team working cannot be understated because the diverse nature and expertise of people working together, towards a common goal, produces a higher quality and more efficiently produced product or service. In the police environment teamwork is obviously of vital importance.

Team working can be a very difficult concept to master. It takes time to understand the process and dynamics of effectively working together, understanding group development, the characteristics of successful teams, how a team solves a problem and how we compensate for the absence of particular roles within the team.

In a management role it is essential to know the theoretical basis for team working as it helps you organise the work of the team. It also enables you to teach and practice team working skills with your staff.

The most successful teams comprise those individuals that understand team working theory and understand the other members of the team. If complete synergy is achieved the best possible outcome to a project will be obtained.

What is a Team?

The words 'team' and 'group' are often used interchangeably, but there is an important distinction between the two. A group of people can be an impromptu gathering of friends, work colleagues or attendees at a course. A team is also a group of people, but the distinction is the interdependence between those people that is geared towards completion of some task or objective. By definition the task or objective is the reason for the existence of the team.

What is Team Membership?

When we join a team and agree to become part of the joint venture to achieve an objective, that acceptance of a common aim and the consent to work with each other depicts membership of that team.

When a team comes together, especially a new team, members bring with them different experiences and skills from teams they have worked with in the past. They also bring with them preferred ways of working. This means that we have to get to know each other and begin to understand how others like to work and behave in the team environment.

There is a natural tension at the formulation of a team between individualism and interdependent working. This arises where individual members will try to understand where their particular approach to team working fits with the other members of the group.

Until the roles and skills inventory are clear a natural tension will exist. When this is resolved, the members will achieve interdependence and will become mutually supportive. This congruence is vital to effective team working. The key is to break down these natural barriers and build a cohesive unit. The acceptance by members that they are one part of the jigsaw will enable interactive and complementary team working. The consequences of not doing so may be fatal to achievement of the overall objective.

We have all had experiences of a group of people coming together, bonding into a team and being really happy in their work. Reflect on those courses that you have attended and have found very stimulating, and those which you did not. Was it about the people on the course and whether there was team bonding?

Often individuals are selected to be part of a team because of their skills and the person selecting them is doing so because they are building a team comprising complementary skills. This is best illustrated by looking at sports teams. There is no sense in having a team of strikers if you do not have players with skills to work mid-field or in goal. The team will be weak in these areas.

The challenge for all managers and team members is to understand the theoretical basis for team working and to use it to make the work place effective, productive and focused.

Team Roles

Dr. Raymond Meredith Belbin, a Cambridge graduate and research fellow at the Cranfield University School of Management carried out extensive research whilst at the Henley Management College and published 'Management Teams - why they succeed or fail', in 1981. Driven by the increasing importance of team-working in organisations at the time, he set out to identify what made a good team, based on research in the UK and Australia. Although the book covered a number of different aspects of team working, it is his description of the team roles that became famous. Belbin found that in successful teams eight different roles could be seen in operation and concluded that when selecting people for a team, filling the eight roles was as important as choosing their technical skills or experiences.

Effective team performance and achievement of organisational goals is key to overall success. Each team type has a valuable contribution to make in generating a cohesive, mutually supportive human 'machine' that is capable of producing good group performance. Teams that incorporate a group of eclectic people are likely to be highly successful.

In simple terms, a well balanced team requires someone who coordinates team effort, a task leader who makes things happen, an individual who comes up with ideas, an evaluator who critically evaluates team activities, a person who seeks out resources, team workers who promote harmony, an implementer who turns strategy into achievable tasks and finally, a person who ensures the job gets done.

The concept works best when used openly within a team or across an organisation. Individual preferences are only useful if they are known to others, so teams can assess who will best fulfill each role. You can use role identification as a form of team-building: it reinforces the fact that everyone brings something to the team.

The eight roles are divided into two generic types:

Extrovert Roles

Outward looking people who are principally concerned with wider issues and how the teamwork will impact on the environment.

Plant

The innovator. Unorthodox, knowledgeable and imaginative, turning out lots of radical ideas. The creative engine-room that needs careful handling to be effective. Individualistic, disregarding practical details or protocol; can become an unguided missile.

Resource Investigator

The extrovert, enthusiastic communicator, with good connections outside the team. Enjoys exploring new ideas, responds well to challenges, and creates this attitude amongst others. Noisy and energetic, quickly loses interest, and can be lazy unless under pressure.

Chair

Calm, self-confident and decisive when necessary. The social leader of the group, ensuring individuals contribute fully, guiding the team to success. Unlikely to bring great intellect or creativity.

Shaper

Energetic, highly-strung, with a drive to get things done. They challenge inertia, ineffectiveness and complacency in the team, but can be abrasive, impatient and easily provoked. Good leaders of start-up or rapid-response teams.

Introvert Roles

Inward-looking people principally concerned with relations and tasks within the group.

Monitor Evaluator

Unemotional, hard headed and prudent. Good at assessing proposals, monitoring progress and preventing mistakes. Dispassionate, clever and discrete. Unlikely to motivate others, takes time to consider, may appear cold and uncommitted. Rarely wrong.

Team Worker

Socially-oriented and sensitive to others. Provides an informal network of communication and support that spreads beyond the formal activities of the team. Often the unofficial or deputy leader, preventing feuding and fragmentation. Concern for team spirit may divert from getting the job done.

Company Worker

The organiser who turns plans into tasks. Conservative, hard-working, full of common sense, conscientious and methodical. Orthodox thinker who keeps the team focused on the tasks in hand. However, lacks flexibility and is unresponsive to new ideas.

Completer Finisher

Makes sure the team delivers. An orderly, anxious perfectionist who worries about everything. Maintains a permanent sense of urgency that can sometimes help and sometimes hinder the team. Good at follow-up and meeting deadlines.

Different roles are important at different times, and the effective team will be aware of who should be centre stage at a given time. You can of course link Belbin roles to personality types, where you will find common words like 'Extrovert' and 'Analytical', but remember that Belbin roles are less definitive. A sales team might be full of extrovert, expressive and energetic people, but someone will still be able to act as the Company Worker or Completer Finisher!

Practical demonstrations have shown the importance of this approach in achieving objectives. A balanced Belbin team has shown consistency in achieving set objectives whilst, just as *'too many cooks spoil the broth'*, teams consisting of groups of Shapers or Completer Finishers are characterised by conflict and failure to achieve the task.

It follows, that awareness of your own preferred team role and others is a major contributor to understanding personal effectiveness in the work place, ensuring group cohesion and increasing overall organisational achievement. This is an essential skill for all leaders and managers.

Team Problem Solving

Even if you have a well balanced team, with all the roles that you need to be effective, it is a good idea to have a structured approach to team working.

If you are familiar with project management you will know how essential it is to have a structured methodology. All of this is designed to have a disciplined approach to achieving the objective. It is not always possible to have such a structured approach to problem solving in the busy policing environment but there are principles you can use to give the team a disciplined approach to dealing with issues in the work place.

(a) Analyse the Situation

After the team has come together there should be a wide ranging discussion between team members to share perceptions of the situation and predicament in which the team finds itself. It should be possible to analyse the equipment, the time available, team member skills, resources and information available to complete the task. Imagine that you have wooden poles, barrels and lengths of rope and you have to build a boat to get across a river. In this scenario it will be useful to spend some time examining the equipment that you have, and identifying whether any of the members have experience of doing this sort of thing before. Ask questions about the task and how long have we to complete it? This analysis will inform the team where you are and what is required right from the start.

(b) Clarify the Objective

Having completed an analysis of the situation it is always very useful to check out that the objective is well defined and every member of the team is clear what you are trying to achieve. If any member is not clear what the team is trying to achieve then cohesion is lost right from the start. There is no sense in building in tensions. If one person believes we are going north and the remainder of the team is planning to go south the team will be working against itself.

(c) Develop Strategies

With the objective clear in everyone's mind it is now time to have a team discussion and draw ideas from each team member on how the task should be completed. Everyone should contribute to this discussion; no view should be dismissed without serious discussion, and quieter members should be invited to put forward their ideas. Sometimes those that have little to say have the key to the door in their back pocket or may have been involved in a similar exercise and have relevant experience that will make this team successful.

(d) Adverse Consequences

During the course of your discussion it is possible you will explore a number of different strategies to complete the task. Each of these will have merits. However, it is important to look closely at the pit falls of the various ideas that have come through. These alternative strategies must be analysed to see which is likely to succeed over those which may have potentially adverse consequences associated with them. Safety of team members may be something that should be taken into consideration and may outweigh other positive aspects of a strategy. Whatever the situation, the team must look closely to see which strategy will work best.

(e) Decision

When the best overall strategy has been determined it is time for the team to make a decision on the how the task will be pursued. It is possible that all members of the team will not agree 100% on the methodology. This means that there will be a need to come to a consensus decision. Essentially, one or more members may not agree with the full details of how things should be done, but they may agree to go along with the overall direction. It is essential that there is a consensus otherwise the team will not be heading in the same direction and it may disintegrate.

To enable the Team Problem Solving model to work there are some critical interpersonal rules that must be adhered to by team members.

Critical Maintenance Skills

(a) Provide a Supportive Climate

A supportive environment is an interactive atmosphere in which team members feel comfortable sharing their ideas with other members. This ensures that everyone is able to contribute ideas that are valued and treated seriously during the course of the discussion to arrive at a solution.

(b) Gate keeping

This is an interpersonal process designed to ensure that all members of the team contribute to the discussion. This involves inviting quieter team members to speak and enabling all to speak uninterrupted.

(c) Active Listening

Part of communication skills is the ability to listen carefully to what others say. Active listening requires the listener to focus on and be engaged with the speaker's ideas. This requires listening to one speaker at a time and understanding what they are saying. The test is being able to summarise what they have said. Dismissive attitudes to ideas surfacing within the team will demonstrate a lack of ability in this area and can contribute to disharmony.

(d) Confronting Issues Constructively

Challenging ideas through simple disagreement will often result in personal conflict or division of the team. Ideas of members must be constructively challenged by ensuring that they are not devalued in a demeaning way and that they are unravelled with dignity and respect. Simply dismissing an idea as unworkable will be perceived as a personal attack and will isolate members, thereby weakening the team synergy.

Team Decision Making

Providing the team has been through the stages of team problem solving and applied the critical maintenance skills a decision should be a natural conclusion. In slow time, an effective decision making process will involve the team gathering as much information as possible and looking for creativity. All team members should fully participate and consider carefully all the alternatives. Providing this is done then a team decision should be arrived at.

It should be possible to reach a decision that every team member will agree to. However, often where time is limited, it will not be possible for every team member to agree 100% with the decision. Where this is the case it is important that the team is not tempted to permit unilateral decision making where one person makes a decision and everyone else signs up to it or a small minority group should not coerce the team into making a particular decision. Similarly, it is not a good idea to allow a vote on the outcome of the decision making process and come up with a 51% majority. If this type of decision making is permitted the team is a long way from agreeing to an effective course of action.

In the ideal world it is desirable to reach unanimity where everyone agrees. Of course, this may not be possible and certain members will not necessarily agree with the full details of the decision that is made. This is not fatal to the efficiency of the decision providing those members are happy to support the course of action.

The Decisions

(a) Unilateral

One person makes a decision for the team.

(b) Majority

At least 51% agree on a decision.

(c) Unanimity

Everyone agrees and there is a discussion of everyone's reasoning so that there is a deeper understanding of the different perspectives of the team.

(d) Concensus

Short of full agreement but sufficient input is obtained from everyone so that all members will support the final decision that has been made.

It should be borne in mind that reaching unanimity will take longer than making any other decision type but the quality of the decision will be guaranteed.

The closer a team comes to reaching unanimity or consensus then true team synergy will be reached.

Personal Team Style

Knowing your own preferred style when working in a team will help you strike a balance between your individualism and team interdependence in the early stages of team building. Your personal style will dictate how you interact with others to arrive at team cohesion.

Similarly, if you are aware of your own personal style, you will be able to spot other personal styles through their typical behaviours and you will be able to take them into account when interpreting their actions. Obviously, if you have knowledge of personal styles you will be able to have expectations of how certain people will behave and you can more easily interpret what they mean.

Being aware of your personal style will enable you to take on roles and tasks that suit you. For example, if you prefer simple, well structured projects then you should take them on rather than those which rely on working through collaboration with other people. Knowing your style enables you to work on team tasks that suit you.

A manager will have to direct (chair) the task but the process should be limited to the theories we have discussed to ensure full team interaction.

Dimensions of Style

We are all unique, there is no one definitive style, but it is clear there are common traits amongst people. For example, research has shown that there are two basic dimensions of style.

(a) Assertiveness

This is the extent to which a person wishes to influence and control the thoughts or actions of others. This style type typically sees people who wish to tell others how things should be; they are task driven, active, confident and ambitious.

People who are not assertive ask others how things should be, are reserved, easygoing, private and deliberate.

(b) Expressiveness

This is the extent to which a person will control his or her emotions and feelings when interacting with others. These people display their emotions, are versatile, sociable and extroverted.

People who are not expressive control their emotions, are dogmatic, controlled and quiet.

Team Member Style Definitions

We define team member style as the way in which an individual expresses their identity when working with a group of people to achieve an objective. Each member style reflects a different combination of assertiveness and expressiveness.

(a) Direct

High Assertiveness, Low Expressiveness:

"This is what needs to be done and this is how we are going to do it."

(b) Spirited

High Assertiveness, High Expressiveness:

"I have a clear vision of how this can be done! We should do this…"

(c) Considerate

Low Assertiveness, High Expressiveness

"What does the rest of the team think?"

(d) Systematic

Low Assertiveness, Low Expressiveness

"If we go about this in a structured and organised manner am sure we can achieve the objective."

You may be wondering whether one style is better than another. The answer is that all four styles are more or less effective in different situations. Your ability to capitalise on the strengths of your preferred style and deal with the potential weaknesses will help you achieve the greatest benefits from your particular style.

A description of the potential strengths and weaknesses of the four team styles follows.

Potential Strengths

Direct
- Can see the big picture
- Sees conflict as constructive
- Risk taker
- Assertive communicator

Spirited
- Enjoys creating new ideas
- Flexible to change
- Praises others for achievements
- Plenty of energy and drive

Considerate
- Listens carefully to others
- Assists others when required
- Encourages team member contributions

- Resolves conflict

Systematic
- Critically analyses information
- Very organised
- Sets high standards
- Focuses on detail

Potential Weaknesses

Direct
- Too critical
- Provides feedback abrasively
- Impatient
- Aggressive

Spirited
- Easily distracted from task
- Deadlines are not important
- Uses disruptive behaviour
- Often deviates from agreed plans

Considerate
- Will not speak out
- Dependent on others
- Too trusting
- Sensitive to criticism

Systematic
- Perfectionist
- Does not like change
- Prefers data over personal relationships
- Inflexible and rigid

What is the difference between Team Styles and Team Roles?

In a successful team **Roles** are clearly defined. These are the different **tasks or responsibilities** that individuals assume to help the team reach its goals. When the roles are well defined team members understand which individuals are responsible for carrying out certain jobs. For example, the leader (Shaper), is often self evident and is the person who provides the drive and direction for the team.

On the other hand, **Styles** are an ***individual's preferred or natural way of behaving*** when working in a team. The distinction is that styles are inherent behaviours while roles can be agreed or assigned. Roles and styles complement each other. Certain team member styles are better suited to certain roles. For example, Direct and Spirited styles are more suited to the extrovert roles while Considerate and Systematic styles are suited to the introverted roles. The relationship between styles and roles follows.

Direct
- Shaper
- Chair

Spirited
- Resource investigator
- Plant

Considerate
- Team worker
- Company worker

Systematic
- Monitor Evaluator
- Completer Finisher

Discover your dominant style

If you would like to discover your own dominant style you can complete the style assessment questionnaire on the ISP Consultancy web site at www.ispconsultancy.com. The results of the assessment will be fed back and then you can insert the scores in the **Team Member Style Profile** boxes below:

Direct	Spirited	Considerate	Systematic

Interpreting your scores

Although you have the ability to use all four team member styles, people tend to have one style they use most frequently. This is your 'dominant' style. Take a look at your Team Member Style Profile.

- A score of 27 or above on any style indicates that style is your dominant style.
- A score of 17 or below on any style indicates that you rarely use this style.
- You may have scored equally on two or more styles. This indicates that you are comfortable using any of those styles, although you may rely on one more than the others.

Team Working

Personal Development Assessment

Consider what you have learned in this chapter about team working and make an assessment of your developmental needs. This will help you to identify and collate, chapter by chapter, areas you need to consider for inclusion in your Personal Action Plan.

1. What **gaps** in your knowledge do you have on team working?

2. What **actions** can you take in the work place or elsewhere to improve knowledge of team working?

3. How do you rate your **skills** in this area?

Rate yourself with a score out of 10.
(10 high, 1 low)

10

Chapter 4

Leadership

Aims

This chapter will introduce you to the fundamental elements of leadership and enable you to:

- **Describe leadership theories**

- **Describe leadership styles**

- **Describe transactional and transformational leadership**

- **Describe your leadership style**

- **Assess your current leadership development needs**

Introduction

Defining leadership has always been a problem. Over 2000 years ago the Greek philosopher Plato wrestled with definitions. More recently, during the 20th Century, a definition of leadership remained elusive but broad themes began to emerge.

(a) 1900 through to 1940s – 'Leaders are born'

The belief was that leaders are born. Those that held positions of power in the political, social and industrial arenas were born with the **traits** of leadership and they were destined to lead and hold positions of power for that fact alone.

(b) 1930s through to 1950s – 'People learn to become leaders'

This period saw the development of the view that identifying traits was not definitive and that the best approach was to identify what leaders do. Therefore leadership was about **behaviours.**

This move away from inherent leadership characteristics led to a belief that leadership behaviours could be learned through training and development. This belief persists today and many organisations see the advantage of training in behavioural leadership.

(c) 1960s to present day – 'Situational Leadership'

Today, there is a strong belief that the style of leadership depends on the situation in which it is required. Effective leaders modify and adapt their leadership behaviours to meet the needs of the situation.

When the behaviour matches the situation a leader is most successful but when it does not the opportunity for good leadership is lost.

It is therefore important to recognise how you can adapt your style to lead effectively in different situations. Before considering the different styles it is important to understand how leadership is defined.

What is Leadership?

Leadership is one of those qualities that is at best confusing and often misunderstood. However, I think we all acknowledge that you can spot leadership when you see it. There are many different views on where leadership comes from and how it develops. In consequence, there are also many different views on what leadership is and how it can be defined.

If we accept the Leadership Trust definition of leadership – 'Leadership is using your *personal power* to win the hearts and minds of people to achieve a common purpose' – then we can relate to our own experiences of leadership. The leader is in a position of power because they can influence people; this is distinct from a person holding a position because of rank or authority. In fact, we see the leader doing three distinct things. Firstly, they are able to influence others to do things that they might not routinely do. Secondly, leaders are able to influence people so that they will follow them and, thirdly, leaders are particularly good in a crisis.

An example of a crisis leader is Sir Winston Churchill. During World War 2, at the height of the Nazi bombing of London when 100,000 people were dying daily, he was able to inspire people to do extraordinary things and to follow him. Churchill had always aspired to be Prime Minister but had to wait until he was 65 years old. Although some thought he would fail, he proved to be the right leader to deal with that extraordinarily difficult moment in history. Why was this?

Churchill was, in many respects, like other leaders. They are people who can create a vision of the future in situations that are difficult or unusual and inspire people to willingly follow them. They do this through demonstrating particular behaviours that appeal to others. The act of leadership is therefore very personal because it flows from the personal traits and actions of the leader. We often experience working with people who possess these skills who are not in a high profile leadership role or position. They may be a unit manager, a team leader or a team member. However, it is easy to recognise that these people are leaders because of their personal traits and how you feel working with and for them.

If we take this a stage further, it is important to remember that all police officers are, by definition, leaders. Wearing a uniform or holding a specific position that delivers a service to the public requires leadership. Attending a road traffic collision, a crime scene or a domestic dispute requires the first officer on scene to demonstrate leadership. It follows that we should not label people as leaders, managers and followers purely because of their position in the organisation. This is far too simplistic and does not recognise that the modern police service is a thinking organisation responding to a complex society. Police officers of all ranks and positions have a leadership role.

Who will lead?

Although we may require police officers to demonstrate leadership, there are those who are more likely to step forward and take the lead. In broad terms, these people know what they want and can articulate it in a way that inspires others to help them achieve their objective. This is a very broad definition and does not take into

Leadership

account that recognised leaders like Winston Churchill, Martin Luther King, Nelson Mandela, Margaret Thatcher and Richard Branson have all found themselves in different situations and have used different leadership behaviours. It is, therefore, difficult to be specific about who will take the lead in different circumstances and what behaviours they will demonstrate.

We can try to produce a list of generic traits that are specific to leadership. For example, we can say that leaders need to be:

- Visionary
- Inspirational
- Good communicators
- Passionate and determined
- Champions of innovation and change
- Builders of alliances
- Able to take action and get results
- Able to demonstrate integrity and courage

This suggests leadership is a simple set of traits that, if identified in a person, will make them an effective leader in any situation. Also, that leadership is an interchangeable skill. For example, assume that military leadership is easily transposed into the policing environment. Is this possible? I think this assumption does not take into account the intrinsic leadership skills required in military and police environments. It is true there may be similar skills possessed by leaders in the two professions but it does not identify the particular behaviours that make each leader successful in their particular field. This, of course applies to other professions like the fire service, ambulance service, business, banking, selling, political parties and companies.

The conclusion we can draw from this simple analysis is that leaders know what they want, know how to articulate it and get people to follow them, it does not mean they are all the same type of people. There are generic traits that are common to leaders, however, individual behaviours dictate how successful the leader will be in a particular situation. Successful leadership, therefore, depends on individual behaviours and different situations.

How do situations define leadership?

Leaders will, providing they have the inclination to lead, emerge at times when a vacuum or a crisis occurs. Events can be quite different from each other and will therefore require the leader to possess unique traits to deal with a particular event. If we have a leader present, success or failure can depend on the behaviours of the leader and how they are applied to the situation. This suggests that leadership, to a great extent, depends on opportunity. As with Winston Churchill, he was the right person for that situation.

There are also other factors that determine how successful a leader will be. Things like the task and how people see the leader in that situation are variables that determine just how successful the leadership will be. This immediately brings to mind those leaders who are good in one situation but not so comfortable in another. The followers will always be aware of this and therefore style is important. Some leaders who are less flexible are likely to be comfortable and successful only in situations that suit their style. Leaders that have developed an ability to work in different ways and vary their style will be able to deal with different situations.

The style that a leader adopts in a situation will depend on the task in hand and whether it is a quick time situation where a directive response is required or a slow time situation where a more nurturing approach is appropriate. It will also depend on the personality of the followers and their expectations in that situation. A team of police officers trained in public order will expect to receive a directive style of leadership when dealing with disorder. A project team comprising of experts are less likely to respond well to directive leadership in a situation that requires a slow time measured response.

Leaders must therefore be aware of the situational relationship between their behaviours, the task and the needs of the followers. Modifying behaviours to meet the situation will be the test of the ability to lead.

We can broadly define four different styles of leadership that demonstrate typical behavioural types:

> **Directive -** This style requires the leader to define the objective, provide direction to the team, allocate roles and specify how to get the job done. Often this is used in a quick time situation or where time is limited and the task is simple.
>
> **Facilitating -** This is a style where the leader provides direction but will spend time selling the idea to the team and gives them a degree of input into how it will be completed. In this way the leader obtains the 'buy in' and commitment from the team. This is a motivational factor that ensures the task is completed.
>
> **Participative -** In this case the leader is prepared to share decision making with the team. The leader facilitates the process and enables the team to work up solutions to a problem or task.
>
> **Delegated -** This style is commonly seen in experienced teams where people are competent and motivated. The leader

gives tasks and responsibility for completion to team members.

Leadership Styles

From Mahatma Gandhi to Jack Welch* and Martin Luther King to Rudolph Giuliani, there are as many leadership styles as there are leaders.

*(*John Francis "Jack" Welch, Jr. (born November 19, 1935) was Chairman and CEO of General Electric between 1981 and 2001. Welch gained a solid reputation for business acumen and unique leadership strategies at GE. He increased GE market capital by over £200 billion. He remains a highly-regarded figure in business circles due to his innovative management strategies and leadership style.)*

Whether you are managing a team at work, captain of your sports team, dealing with a family crisis or leading a major corporation, your leadership style is, as we have seen, crucial to success. Consciously, or subconsciously, you will use some of the leadership styles featured above, at least some of the time. Understanding these leadership styles and their impact can help you develop and adapt your own leadership style so you become a more effective leader.

Understanding Leadership Styles

So far we have discussed leadership broadly and defined four main styles. However, academics have distilled these into sub-categories attributing different characteristics to each one. To provide perspective on the complexity of these styles we look at ten different definitions here:

(a) Autocratic Leadership

Autocratic leadership is an extreme form of *transactional leadership (see below for explanation)*, where the leader has absolute power over his or her employees or team. Employees and team members have little opportunity for making suggestions, even if these would be in the team's interest.

Most people tend to resent being treated like this and, in consequence, this style of leadership usually leads to high levels of sickness absence and staff turnover. However, for some routine and unskilled jobs this style can remain effective where the advantages of control outweigh the disadvantages.

(b) Bureaucratic Leadership

Bureaucratic leaders work 'by the book', ensuring that their staff follow procedures exactly. This is an appropriate style for work involving serious safety risks, such as working with machinery, with toxic substances or at heights, or where large sums of money are involved, such as cash-handling.

(c) Charismatic Leadership

Charismatic leadership can appear similar to *transformational* leadership (see below), in that the leader injects huge doses of enthusiasm into the team, and is very energetic in driving others forward. However, charismatic leaders tend to believe more in themselves than in their team. This can create a risk that a project, or even an entire organisation, might collapse if the leader were to leave. In the eyes of their followers, success is tied up with the presence of the charismatic leader. As such, charismatic leadership carries great responsibility and needs long-term commitment from the leader.

(d) Democratic or Participative Leadership

Although a democratic leader will make the final decision, he or she invites other members of the team to contribute to the decision-making process. This not only increases job satisfaction by involving employees or team members in what is going on, but it also helps to develop people's skills. Employees and team members feel in control of their own destiny, such as the promotion they desire, and are motivated to work hard by more than just a financial reward.

As participation takes time, this approach can lead to things happening more slowly, but often the end result is better. The approach can be most suitable where team working is essential, and quality is more important than productivity.

(e) Laissez-faire Leadership

This French phrase means 'leave it be' and is used to describe a leader who leaves his or her colleagues to get on with their work. It can be effective if the leader monitors what is being achieved and communicates this back to the team regularly. Most often, laissez-faire leadership works for teams in which the individuals are very experienced and skilled self-starters. Unfortunately, it can also refer to situations where managers are not exerting sufficient control. With an inexperienced team this can be highly undesirable.

(f) People-Oriented or Relations-Oriented Leadership

This style of leadership is the opposite of task-oriented leadership (see below); the leader is totally focused on organising, supporting and developing the people in the team. As a participative style, it tends to lead to good teamwork and creative collaboration. In practice, most leaders use both task-oriented and people-oriented styles of leadership.

(g) Servant Leadership

This term, coined by Robert Greenleaf (1904-1990), founder of the Servant Leadership movement, described a leader as someone who is often not formally recognised as such. When someone, at any level within an organisation, leads simply by virtue of meeting the needs of the team, they are a 'servant leader'. In many ways, servant leadership is a form of democratic leadership, as the whole team is making decisions.

Supporters of the servant leadership model suggest it is an important way ahead in a world where values and ethics are increasingly important, in which servant leaders achieve power on the basis of their values and ideals. Others believe that in competitive leadership situations, people practicing servant leadership will often find themselves left behind by leaders using other leadership styles.

(h) Task-Oriented Leadership

A highly task-oriented leader focuses only on getting the job done, and can be quite autocratic. He or she will actively define the work and the roles required, put structures in place, plan, organise and monitor. However, as task-oriented leaders spare little thought for the well-being of their teams, this approach can suffer many of the flaws of autocratic leadership, with difficulties in motivating and retaining staff.

(i) Transactional Leadership

This style of leadership is characterised by team members agreeing to obey their leader totally. The 'transaction' is usually that the organisation pays the team members in return for their effort and compliance. The leader has a right to punish the team members if their work does not meet the required standard.

Team members can do little to improve their job satisfaction under transactional leadership. The leader gives team members control of their income/reward by using incentives that encourage higher standards or greater productivity. Alternatively, a transactional leader may manage by exception, whereby, rather than rewarding better work, corrective action is taken if the required standards are not met.

Transactional leadership is really just a way of managing rather than a true leadership style as the focus is on short-term tasks. It has serious limitations for knowledge-based or creative work, but remains a common style in many organisations.

(j) Transformational Leadership

This charismatic style of leadership is particularly popular with current police thinking and is what many police forces are aspiring to emulate and develop in their staff at all levels. For this reason, it is important to your personal development that you understand what transformational leadership is, what traits you would expect to see in someone who demonstrates this style of leadership and how it differs from transactional leadership.

As we have seen, transactional leadership focuses on the transaction, or agreement, that exists between leader and followers. The relationship exists because the leader agrees with the followers what is required of them and specifies the rewards they will receive on completion of the task. This can be a simple employer/employee contract or other incentives like bonus payments. This style is more akin to management than leadership but is essential in any organisation because it ensures routine work is completed satisfactorily. On the other hand, transformational leaders are people that take leadership to a higher level.

Transformational leaders are thoroughbred leaders who are characterised by the following:

(a) They have a powerful and compelling vision of the future

(b) They are highly visible and spend a great deal of time communicating

(c) They are inspirational and obtain support from followers to embrace and share the vision

(d) They are passionate about what they want and are determined to succeed

(e) They motivate others to go to extraordinary lengths and do things that they would not normally do or thought possible

(f) They are champions of innovation and change who encourage followers to problem solve and experiment with new ideas and methods

(g) They focus on followers' development by empowering them and aligning their personal goals with those of the organisation

(h) They build strong alliances internally and externally

(i) They are focused on taking action and getting results

(j) They are noted for consistency because of their integrity and courage to take risks

[Bernard M. Bass and Ronald E. Riggio (2006) have identified these transforming traits as four main components of transformational leadership: idealised influence (charisma), inspirational leadership, intellectual stimulation and individualised consideration. *Idealised influence* and *inspirational leadership* are where leaders are able to get their followers to identify with them because of their natural ability to define a clear vision and how it will be achieved. They also identify with their high standards, confidence and determination. *Intellectual stimulation* enables followers to be creative and *individualised consideration* identifies a coaching and mentoring approach to develop followers. Further reading: Transformational Leadership second edition ISBN 0-8058-4762-6]

From this list of transformational leadership traits we can see that this type of leadership is very powerful and compelling. It is rarely seen naturally in people but through understanding and adjustment of behaviours we can individually improve our personal performance. If we accept that leadership can be learned and that the situation is important, the impact we have on people can be considerable.

The other important point is that leadership is not solely the domain of the people at the top. As already stated, every constable is a leader. We can take this further and recognise that everyone, police officers, police staff, PCSOs, special constables, volunteers and anyone else that works for the organisation is a leader.

A transforming organisation wants to inspire everyone to be a problem solver and experiment with new ideas and methods. It also encourages people to develop themselves and help them to align their objectives with the vision of the organisation. They are inspired to take action, get results, have a high degree of integrity and are not criticised for making mistakes. Mistakes are seen as an opportunity to learn and improve the organisation. As we have seen, this is distinct from transactional leadership which, although effective in getting the job done, does not transform the organisation and improve performance. A transforming organisation has a reciprocal effect on everyone by preventing stagnation and creating a sense of well being where people are happy, perform better and believe that their individual effort is worth it.

Transformational leaders at their best

Crisis

In times of stress or catastrophe, transformational leaders are very effective at taking the initiative and clearly articulating a vision of the future. They communicate it in such a way that people will be inspired and motivated to a time beyond the emergency.

On such occasions they clearly display that they are in charge by exhibiting behaviours that demonstrate they are concerned, calm and decisive. These situations draw out the leaders who are charismatic and appeal to people who may have lost their way. After the 11th September 2001 attack on the World Trade Center in New York, Rudolph Giuliani, the City's Mayor, demonstrated transformational leadership by immediately being visible, vocal and demonstrating personal concern for what had occurred.

He visited the disaster site minutes after the attack and in the days and weeks that followed he gave high profile press conferences to communicate what he was doing and how the response to the crisis was progressing. He also attended many of the funerals that took place. By demonstrating he was in control through his openness and compassion for people he inspired them to see beyond the disaster. He has since written about the optimism of leadership as an important behaviour:

> *"Once the leader gives up, then everyone else gives up, and there's no hope…It's up to a leader to instill confidence, to believe in his judgment and in his people even when they no longer believe in themselves. Sometimes, the optimism of a leader is grounded in something only he*

> *knows – the situation isn't as dire as people think for reasons that will eventually become clear. But sometimes the leader has to be optimistic simply because if he isn't nobody else will be. And you've got at least to try to fight back, no matter how daunting the odds."(Giuliani Leadership, p.298)*

This high profile leadership is important in a crisis but, as Giuliani states, it is important in all situations, even when things are not as bad as people perceive them to be.

Communication is an important vehicle for setting out your vision and what you intend to do about it. Winston Churchill did this extremely well. During the Second World War the Nazi war machine marched through Europe and between 10th and 26th May in 1940 Hitler's army crushed the Netherlands, Luxembourg and France, and trapped the British Expeditionary Force of 200,000 on the beaches at Dunkirk. On 4th June 1940 Churchill addressed the House of Commons and made clear his vision for the future and what he intended to do:

> *"Against this loss of over 30,000 men, we can set a far heavier loss certainly inflicted upon the enemy. But our losses in material are enormous. We have perhaps lost*

one-third of the men we lost in the opening days of the battle of 21st March, 1918, but we have lost nearly as many guns, nearly one thousand- and all our transport, all the armoured vehicles that were with the Army in the north. This loss will impose a further delay on the expansion of our military strength.

I have, myself, full confidence that if all do their duty, if nothing is neglected, and if the best arrangements are made, as they are being made, we shall prove ourselves once again able to defend our Island home, to ride out the storm of war, and to outlive the menace of tyranny, if necessary for years, if necessary alone. At any rate, that is what we are going to try to do.

We shall go on to the end, we shall fight in France, we shall fight on the seas and oceans, we shall fight with growing confidence and growing strength in the air, we shall defend our island, whatever the cost may be, we shall fight on the beaches, we shall fight on the landing grounds, we shall fight in the fields and in the streets, we shall fight in the hills; we shall never surrender, and even if,

> *which I do not for a moment believe, this island or a large part of it were subjugated and starving, then our Empire beyond the seas, armed and guarded by the British fleet, would carry on the struggle, until, in God's good time, the New World, with all its power and might, steps forth to the rescue and the liberation of the old."*

As a charismatic leader Churchill is well known for his outstanding oratory skills. Not only did he write his own speeches but he practiced delivering them. For every one minute of speech he would practice his delivery for two hours. In his speeches he was very honest about the reality of the situation and shared the worst details, which he clearly did in this speech. However, he always gave hope by stating what had to be done and drawing people into the task. He created a sense of duty and individual responsibility to pull together for the benefit of everyone.

He was clear what 'we' had to do:

> *"I have, myself, full confidence that if **all** do their duty, if nothing is neglected, and if the best arrangements are made, as they are being made, **we** shall prove ourselves once again able to defend*

> ***our** Island home, to ride out the storm of war."* (emphasis added)

He was also very specific about what had to be done. Again, there was no lack of clarity about the stark reality of the situation. In this case 'we' are to fight:

> *"We shall go on to the end, we shall fight in France, we shall fight on the seas and oceans, we shall fight with growing confidence and growing strength in the air, we shall defend our island, whatever the cost may be, we shall fight on the beaches, we shall fight on the landing grounds, we shall fight in the fields and in the streets, we shall fight in the hills."*

Although he states what is to be done, he does not specify in this speech how it will be done; like all good leaders, he leaves that to the experts, in this case the military.

It all sounds rather grave; a terrible situation, we are all going to have to pull our weight and we are required to fight. But he does finally give a picture of hope:

> *"...even if, which I do not for a moment believe, this island or a large part of it were subjugated and*

starving, then our Empire beyond the seas, armed and guarded by the British fleet, would carry on the struggle, until, in God's good time, the New World, with all its power and might, steps forth to the rescue and the liberation of the old."

This speech demonstrates just how a leader can grasp the moment in a crisis and be charismatic. A transformational leader, despite the size and apparent impossibility of the situation, can inspire people and make them enthusiastic about the task ahead. They are also very energetic in motivating others to take action and pull together. Their followers try to emulate the positive attitudes and the vision of the leader. As such, transformational leadership carries great responsibility and needs long-term commitment from the leader.

Normality

Transformational leaders have great strength in times of crisis but they are also extremely effective in times of relative normality. Their greatest strength is a strong vision of the future and the ability to communicate it passionately. Unlike transactional leaders, who tend to deal with the here and now by providing solutions to immediate problems, the transformational leader operates at a higher level and is concerned with the common good by preparing followers for the challenges of the future. The natural desire to be prepared for the future by putting in place appropriate mechanisms enables a transforming organisation to anticipate and deal with a potential crisis. Also, by encouraging the work force to constantly search for problems and be creative ensures that responses to changing situations are available.

In addition, encouraging followers to be problem solvers intellectually stimulates and refreshes them. As a result they are less likely to suffer from boredom, cynicism and a general feeling of being burnt out in their jobs. The fact that transformers are more likely to seek out ideas and solutions from their followers also gives them a sense of value and responsibility for the direction of the organisation. Similarly, the personal focus of the transformer can assist in identifying individual needs and recognising those people who want to move forward more energetically than others and tailor their individual contribution and personal development.

Another factor is the cohesion created by individuals who are well motivated. The interaction of people who are enthusiastic creates a sense of importance and value to individual contributions. This obviously benefits the organisation and negates any boredom and negative attitudes.

Summary

It is clear that transformational leaders are effective in both stepping up to deal with a crisis and for preparing an organisation to respond to a crisis. Both situations apply to policing and it is therefore important to a transforming organisation, that police leaders (all staff) recognise the importance of demonstrating leadership behaviours in the work place.

Perhaps the most important thing for a transforming organisation is the need for the leader at the top to be in post for a period of time that will enable change to be made. Transforming an organisation, in the way that has been described, requires sustained effort and the success of leadership will be demonstrated when the organisation embodies the leader. When local people ascribe the personality of the force to the chief officer the transformation is complete. M. R. Haberfield in her book *Police Leadership* describes the time when she visited the Charleston Police Department (USA) and was taking a taxi from the air port to the police HQ. The taxi driver commented on her destination and the local police chief saying, "Yes, I know Reuben. Please say hello from me – Reuben *is* the Charleston Police department."

One word of warning - integrity

Transformational leadership can be very powerful because it frees up employees through encouraging innovation and creativity. It also transcends individual needs and focuses on the greater common good. The fact that transformational leaders encourage self determination means they are less critical of people than perhaps a transactional leader would be, meaning there is less control. This lack of control can distort the morality of how things are achieved. Staff can begin to believe in an organisational ethic that does not necessarily match the views they held before the transformation. This can lead to a change of moral perspectives and the ethical backbone of the organisation can become corrupt.

There have been examples of this occurring in small police units down through the years. A charismatic transformational leader in a specialist unit can, sometimes unwittingly, encourage staff to push the boundaries of ethical behaviour. Staff may adopt corrupt practices to achieve the leader's vision because they feel it is acceptable to the organisation. These corrupt practices have been referred to as 'noble cause corruption'. This is a way of trying to justify corrupt practice by saying, in the name of justice, the end justifies the means. Eventually these practices will discredit the leader and the organisation.

The leader can also wittingly create an unethical environment and get the staff to believe this is acceptable to the organisation. Hitler was a transformational leader and the morality of what he was doing, although wrong, was seen as necessary and morally right by the majority of his followers.

As you develop your transformational leadership, be certain you understand the power of this style of leadership and recognise the impact it can have on you and your staff.

(k) Situational Leadership

While the transformational leadership approach is often highly effective, there is no one right way to lead or manage that suits all situations. To choose the most effective approach for you, you must consider:

- The skill levels and experience of your team
- The work involved (routine or new and creative)
- The organisational environment (stable or radically changing, conservative or adventurous)
- You own preferred or natural style.

A good leader will switch instinctively between styles according to the people and work they are dealing with. This is referred to as situational leadership. For example, the manager of a small factory trains and develops new machine operatives using a bureaucratic style to ensure operatives know the procedures that achieve the right standards of product quality and workplace safety. The same manager may adopt a more participative style of leadership when working on production line improvement with his or her team of supervisors.

Your Leadership Style

Knowing your own preferred leadership style when working with your team will enable you to adapt your style to deal with different situations. Your personal style will dictate how you interact with others to make your team productive and efficient.

Similarly, if you are aware of your own personal style, you will be able to spot other personal styles through typical behaviours and you will be able to take them into account when interpreting their actions. Obviously, if you have knowledge of typical different personal styles you will have expectations of how certain people will behave and you can more easily interpret what they mean.

Being aware of your personal style will enable you to put emphasis on the appropriate style for different situations. Different scenarios may dictate that more transactional, rather than transformational, leadership behaviours will be required.

Dimensions of Style

As we have seen in Chapter 3 on Team Working, we are all unique and there is no one definitive leadership style but, as we have seen, it is clear there are common traits amongst people. For example, research has shown that there are two basic dimensions of style.

(a) Assertiveness

This is the extent to which a person wishes to influence and control the thoughts or actions of others. This style type typically sees people who wish to tell others how things should be; they are task driven, active, confident and ambitious.

People who are not assertive ask others how things should be, are reserved, easygoing, private and deliberate.

(b) Expressiveness

This is the extent to which a person will control his or her emotions and feelings when interacting with others. These people display their emotions, are versatile, sociable and extroverted.

People who are not expressive control their emotions, are dogmatic, controlled and quiet.

Leadership Style Definitions

We define leadership style as the way in which an individual expresses their identity when working with a group of people to achieve an objective. Each leadership style reflects a different combination of assertiveness and expressiveness.

(a) Direct

High Assertiveness, Low Expressiveness:

"I know what needs to be done and here's how we should do it."

(b) Spirited

High Assertiveness, High Expressiveness:

"I have a great idea! What if we…"

(c) Considerate

Low Assertiveness, High Expressiveness

"What does everyone else think?"

(d) Systematic

Low Assertiveness, Low Expressiveness

"With careful planning and organisation, I know we can meet our deadline."

Discover Your Dominant Style

If you would like to discover your own dominant style you can complete the style assessment questionnaire on the ISP Consultancy web site at www.ispconsultancy.com. The results of the assessment will be fed back and then you can insert the scores in the **Leadership Style Profile** boxes below:

Direct	Spirited	Considerate	Systematic

Interpreting Your Scores

Although you have the ability to use all four leadership styles, people tend to have one style they use most frequently. This is your 'dominant' style. Take a look at your Leadership Style Profile.

- A score of 16 or above on any style indicates that style is your dominant style.
- A score of 10 or below on any style indicates that you rarely use this style.
- You may have scored equally on two or more styles. This indicates that you are comfortable using any of those styles, although you may rely on one more than the others.

You may be wondering whether one style is better than another. The answer is that all four styles are more or less effective in different situations. Your ability to capitalise on the strengths of your preferred style and deal with the trouble spots will help you achieve the greatest benefits from your particular style.

Potential Strengths and Weaknesses

Direct

Most Effective in crisis or rapidly changing situations in which bold action or quick decisions are required.

Less Effective in situations requiring careful planning and where tact and sensitivity to others feelings is required.

Spirited

Most Effective in situations in which people need to be motivated to develop fresh, innovative ideas.

Less Effective in urgent situations in which deadlines must be met and in situations in which long-term planning is vital.

Systematic

Most Effective in situations calling for careful, long-term planning, accuracy and objective analysis.

Less Effective in situations requiring quick decision making or flexibility because of ambiguity or interpersonal conflict.

Considerate

Most Effective in sensitive situations requiring patience, tact and diplomacy.

Less Effective in situations requiring quick adjustments because of unforeseen changes and situations in which the need to take charge of others is crucial.

Leadership

Personal Development Assessment

Consider what you have learned in this chapter about leadership and make an assessment of your developmental needs. This will help you to identify and collate, chapter by chapter, areas you need to consider for inclusion in your Personal Action Plan.

1. What **gaps** in your knowledge do you have on leadership?

2. What **actions** can you take in the work place or elsewhere to improve knowledge of leadership?

3. How do you rate your **skills** in this area?

Rate yourself with a score out of 10.
(10 high, 1 low)

10

Chapter 5

Management

Aims

This chapter will introduce you to the fundamental elements of management and enable you to:

- **Describe the role of a manager**

- **Describe the management link between organisation and team**

- **Describe the five management skills**

- **Assess your current management skills development needs**

Introduction

So far, in previous chapters, we have examined the key elements of personality, team working and leadership. All of these are the tools to do the job of leading people with the objective of getting the job done.

We have considered different leadership styles and identified when these styles are most effective. In particular, we have looked at transactional and transformational leadership. Although the latter is what many police organisations aspire to achieve there is always a need to make sure the job gets done. This is where, despite the transformations taking place, there will always be a need for transactional leaders who can manage people.

The previous chapters do not necessarily provide a framework that you can use to make sense of all the theory. This chapter is intended to provide some clarity about how people should be managed in the workplace to make sure we are not swirling around in the theoretical ether without a sense of direction. It will also provide a bench mark from which you can distinguish between transactional, transformational and the other styles of leadership. You may also be able to use the framework provided to experiment and develop your own personal style as determined from the results of the style questionnaire.

If you are aspiring to get into a specialist department you will find this useful in understanding how people should be managed in a balanced way to meet the needs of the people and organisation. If you are seeking promotion this will give you focus on what you are trying to achieve as a situational leader. If you are already a situational leader you may find this a useful review mechanism to refocus your activities which are often disrupted by operational imperatives.

Role of Manager

Simply put, the role of a manager is getting work done through others. However, this simple definition has taken on different meanings down through history.

In the industrial revolution a manager was given almost complete control of the people they supervised. They had sole responsibility for hiring, firing and discipline.

This position changed somewhat with the progression of more scientific approaches to management and strategic planning, influencing the way in which the work was done to meet corporate needs. In addition, the growth of unions has provided much more restriction on the control of labour, industrial law and the health and safety issues. The result has been to restrict the influence of the manager over members of staff.

We have seen the growth of human resource departments, legal departments, union consultation, health and safety legislation, diversity, under performance, performance review and a litigious culture which has made the whole issue of managing people in the work place increasingly more complex.

Despite this, one thing that has not changed is the constant demand for productivity through people. So, although there are complex issues for the manager to understand and deal with, the task of inspiring the work force remains the same. The manager has to get the best from them. The police environment constantly requires even more productivity and Home Office scrutiny has never been more intrusive.

The skills of the manager today require good communication skills with diverse groups inside and outside the organisation, problem solving skills, creativity and imagination, critical thinking, and the ability to develop employees.

What must be recognised is that managers in the modern world who are promoted into these responsible positions cannot be expected to know everything at the outset to get the job done effectively.

It is essential to know the vocational technicalities of the job but it is absolutely essential that managers manage the staff they have working for them. These are essential skills and managers must not hide behind the technicalities of the job, becoming risk adverse, through failing to lead and manage people effectively.

New managers must face some unfamiliar issues, such as how to direct the group, how to let go of day-to-day tasks while still maintaining enough knowledge to guide the work, and how to maintain good relations with friends who now work for them. Making the transition to a supervisor requires a shifting of attitudes, not just an increase in knowledge.

Situational Leadership/Management

The primary role of the manager is to provide a link between the senior management of the organisation and the employees, and is accountable for getting the work done. In addition, the manager is responsible for the well being of the staff and for their own personal development.

The manager has to understand and translate the strategic direction set by the senior leaders in the organisation. The skill of the manager will determine just how the organisational vision is translated effectively into individual and team

Management

tasks to get the work done. This situational leadership/management is fundamental to achieving the organisational objectives.

In order to achieve the organisational vision and get the work done in the most effective way the manager will need to organise the work, develop staff, manage and drive performance formally and informally, and manage relationships with several teams inside and outside the team.

The Management Framework

The key elements of the management framework are:

- guiding the work
- organising the work
- developing staff
- managing and driving performance
- managing relations

(a) Guiding the Work

Guiding the work involves understanding the strategic direction of the organisation and translating it into actionable plans for the team.

The manager must have a broad picture and understanding of the organisation to enable them to guide the team in the right direction. Employees know that a manager is the link between them and senior management. They will look to them to provide direction on where the organisation is going. Without a sense of direction employees become confused and feel undervalued. Sometimes giving employees organisational direction is uncomfortable because of resistance but it is key to effective management.

(b) Organising the Work

Organising the work involves assigning people, equipment and tasks to meet work goals.

The manager must be constantly reassessing the direction of the organisation and assigning work appropriately. In doing so they must keep the needs of the staff in mind and ensure they fit with the organisational needs. This takes real people skills, but no matter what decisions are made the staff need to know the manager has taken them into account and considered their needs.

Often the manager will need to recognise that individuals will have more expertise in certain areas than they do. There should never be any resistance to engaging experts and using them appropriately to achieve team goals. The manager's role is to maintain an overview and constantly learn from others to facilitate the forward direction of the organisation.

As part of the hierarchical structure of the organisation the manager must recognise that informal networks and relationships exist. Providing these are geared to assisting the formalised management structures and are not working against the cohesion of the organisation, it is important to use these for the benefit of the team and the strategic direction.

(c) Developing Your Staff

Developing your staff involves being aware of their abilities and actively helping them to develop their skill level.

The important component here is knowledge of each employee and understanding their skills, abilities, needs and personality. The biggest barrier to accumulating this knowledge and focusing on staff development is time. Managers are almost always absorbed by the team priorities and often take on tasks themselves just to get them done.

The secret to making quality time for staff development is delegation. By delegating work this frees up the manager to have time for staff issues and their own development.

Delegation also allows the manager to set the parameters of the work and to choose an individual with the right skills or development needs to take it on. Coaching and guidance then follow with the manager remaining responsible for the work. In doing so, it is important that the responsibility for training lies with the manager.

(d) Managing and Driving Performance

Managing performance involves removing the obstacles to better performance so that employees can meet both their own objectives as well as those of the organisation.

Managing employee's performance is often dependent on obstacles in the work place and inherent within the employee. An effective manager must be aware of both. It follows that coaching of employees to achieve their true potential is vital and should include an assessment of the employee's true potential and instilling in them the confidence that they can achieve more.

The manager must ensure that they tell the employee what is required of them and expectations must be understood by the employee. Keeping employees involved in reviewing and tracking their own performance will increase their commitment. In addition, self assessment will enable an employee to keep their performance on track. With the appropriate support an employee will perform effectively.

(e) Managing Relations

Managing relations involves developing and maintaining good relationships with other teams so that the manager's employees and the organisation meet their goals.

Teams within organisations should not operate within a vacuum. In fact, the more those teams become connected, internally and externally, the more likely they and the organisation will be successful. Like other skills, managing relations should be guided by the strategic direction of the organisation as it puts other teams on common ground and provides a reliable platform for decision making.

Communication is vital to building relations and, although time consuming, it should be frequent and on-going. This will keep units connected and therefore available to provide support and expertise should it be necessary.

Summary

It is suggested that this framework is used to help build a structured approach to your development. Whatever role, or position, you are targeting, structure is important to provide focus. In many respects these elements are good for self-management just as they are for managing other people. Reflect on this suggestion and consider how you might deal with this as you make your self assessment at the end of this chapter and structure your development plan as outlined in Chapter 10.

Management

Personal Development Assessment

Consider what you have learned in this chapter about management skills and make an assessment of your developmental needs. This will help you to identify and collate, chapter by chapter, areas you need to consider for inclusion in your Personal Action Plan.

1. What **gaps** in your knowledge do you have on management skills?

2. What **actions** can you take in the work place or elsewhere to improve knowledge of management skills?

3. How do you rate your **skills** in this area?

    Rate yourself with a score out of 10.
       (10 high, 1 low)

10

Chapter 6

Matching to Core Competencies

Aims

This chapter will introduce you to the fundamental elements of matching to core competencies and enable you to:

- **Describe core competencies**

- **Describe matching to core competencies**

- **Describe the STAR methodology**

- **Assess your current matching development needs**

Matching to Core Competencies

Introduction

The current police service competencies are to be found in the *Skills for Justice* 'Integrated Competency Framework.' This consists of a set of national standards and guidelines that enable police forces to improve the consistency and quality of performance in roles and ranks across England, Wales and Northern Ireland.

The framework consists of three key areas:

- (a) National Competency Framework (NCF)
- (b) National Occupational Standards (NOS)
- (c) Performance and Development Review (PDR)

These three areas have been integrated and form the basis for recruitment of police constables, training, staff selection, staff development and inspections by Her Majesty's Inspector of Constabulary. The NCF provides competencies that define what is required in different roles and ranks and the PDR provides the mechanism for measuring performance and formulating plans to address development issues. The NOS are a set of standards that define the quality of work required in particular roles and ranks and can be used to assist in measuring performance. The NOS requirement

Matching to Core Competencies

for Respect for Race and Diversity can be seen at Appendix 1 and is discussed in Chapter 8.

The National Competency Framework is intended to give police forces a clear picture of what is required of personnel, police and police staff, in carrying out their duties. This is achieved by defining activities and behaviours required in role and rank profiles.

There is an Activities Library of 131 activities that define what is required. Each of these activities is linked to 18 core responsibility areas, for example, intelligence, police operations, custody and prosecution. Each of these activities is also linked into the NOS which sets the performance standards.

There is also a Behavioural Library that consists of 30 behaviours describing how the particular jobs are required to be done. For example, leadership, working with others and achieving results are defined and broken down into two or three categories describing the complexity required in each.

The focus for these activities and behaviours is the rank and role. Each rank has a set of generic competencies that are required for effective performance and anyone aspiring to that rank will have to be able to demonstrate the competencies. Recruiting constables is a good example; every recruit has to be able to

Matching to Core Competencies

evidence that they possess the skills required through the National Recruitment Model (NRM) selection process before they can be appointed as a constable. If an individual aspires to become a detective constable or a mounted section officer then the generic competencies will be applicable but there may also be additional skills that are role specific. The same applies to the rank of sergeant. There are generic competencies but there are also role specific competencies for roles like detective sergeant and custody sergeant.

The skills required in ranks and roles have been rigorously researched and validated. However, police forces have a degree of flexibility in how they wish to use them. They will generally stick to the generic competencies for ranks but there may be variation across forces about what they require in role profiles. Either way, police forces are free to use these rank and role profiles to capture the required style of policing or direction that the force is going. Consequently, candidates need to be aware what the force is looking for and ensure they meet the requirements of the competencies.

It follows that in all police selection processes you must expect to be tested against a set of core competencies that have been determined for the rank or role to which you are applying. Each competency defines the competency area (e.g. Team Working), sets a standard and has

Matching to Core Competencies

positive indicators that specify what behaviours are expected by an individual holding that rank or rolek and a set of negative indicators that describe the behaviours that are not acceptable.

The selection board process is designed to test **what** and **how** you do things in particular circumstances. The generic competencies for constable, sergeant and inspector follow:

Constable
- Community and Customer Focus
- Effective Communication
- Personal Responsibility
- Problem Solving
- Resilience
- Respect for Race and Diversity
- Team Working

Sergeant
- Maximising Potential
- Respect for Race and Diversity
- Community and Customer Focus
- Effective Communication
- Problem Solving
- Planning and Organising
- Resilience

Inspector
- Maximising Potential
- Respect for Race and Diversity
- Community and Customer Focus
- Effective Communication

Matching to Core Competencies

- Problem Solving
- Planning and Organising
- Strategic Perspective
- Personal Responsibility

You need to know what the core competencies are for the role, whether you are applying for a specialist post or promotion, and you have to produce evidence to demonstrate that you have the required skills. It is also important to recognise that some police forces will be looking for you to evidence the competencies of the target role or rank and not just what you have done in the past in your current role. So, if you are applying for a post on CID or roads policing you will have to collect evidence of things you have done in the past that demonstrate you have the skills to meet the demands of those roles in the future.

It is important to make sure you have examples of what you have done and how you did them before you fill out the application form or attend a formal interview. If you do not, then you must work this out before you commence your preparation. This is the first step in your preparation for the process.

As with all interviews and tests you should be self aware and have a thorough understanding of your personality profile as described in Chapter 2.

The ability to present your skills effectively is fundamental to the application stage and the formal interview. The selection process is generally designed to draw out whether you have:

(a) The skills required of the role/rank

(b) The style of policing preferred by the force.

(c) The direction of the force

The style is often determined by the approach to policing articulated in the force policing plan. This will be dealt with in Chapter 7.

Matching to Core Competencies

This raises the whole issue of how you match yourself to the core competencies and the force strategy. Both are extremely important to the selection process and how you prepare yourself is important to ensure that you can demonstrate the skills required.

As a first step towards passing the test of your suitability for selection it makes sense to look very carefully at the skills required for the job and check whether you match them or not. For example, there is little point applying for a job that requires a university degree in mathematics

Matching to Core Competencies

if you do not even have a General Certificate of Secondary Education (GCSE) in the subject!

How to Prepare

By way of illustration look at the competencies for the rank constable. For the rank of constable there are seven core competencies. These are the skills that have been determined as essential for the role and will be tested during the selection process. To make sure you are fully prepared you should undertake the following preparatory work on the competencies:

> Know and understand the **Definition** of the core competency.
>
> And, in each one:
>
> - Understand the **Level Required** (standard)
> - Examine the **Positive Indicators** (behaviours)
> - Recognise what constitutes **Negative Indicators** (behaviours)

When you have done this you will need to think of an example that demonstrates the competency. This is often not an easy task. The best way to tackle this is to think of an experience you have had and then work back towards the competency. The following example of team working illustrates the process.

Example: Team Working

Firstly…

You are able to recall a time when… *'I had to organise a competitive team hike across the Brecon Beacons in Wales. It was particularly hazardous for the competitors and organisation of the event required a team of 10 people. There was a whole raft of different things to be completed to ensure the smooth and safe running of the event, including a close relationship with the emergency services in the event that anything went wrong…'*

Secondly…

Examine the **Positive Indicators** under the team working competency and try to find evidence of as many of them as you can from the team task you had to complete. You may, for example, be able to find enough to demonstrate the following:

- Understand own role in a team
- Make time to get to know people
- Offers help to other people
- Develops mutual trust and confidence in others
- Willingly takes on unpopular or routine tasks

Matching to Core Competencies

- Contribute to team objectives no matter what the direct personal benefit may be
- Acknowledge there is often a need to be in more than one team

Thirdly...

Check that you do not display any **Negative Indicators.** You should not display any negative indicators as these will suggest to the assessors that you do not possess the necessary skill.

Fourthly...

Look at the **Required Level** and see if the skills you have displayed reach the standard:

'Works effectively as a team member and helps build relationships within it. Actively helps and supports others to achieve team goals'

If you do, you have just identified your skills in that area and become more self-aware.

Repeat this for all the competencies and you will then have a good understanding of each competency and what skills you have in that area. You will then have matched yourself against the skills required. You may also have identified areas where you have particular strengths and those where there is scope for development.

Matching to Core Competencies

Having trouble matching yourself?

For many candidates this may not appear as simple as it seems. It is sometimes difficult to think of specific examples of the required behaviours. This difficulty is often experienced when completing the application form and when answering questions at the selection board.

If you are finding the matching process difficult and you are unable to come up with an example of your behaviour under a particular competency, try the following approach. For the purposes of illustration consider the competency Problem Solving and the following four steps.

1. Take a close look at the **Required Level**. You will notice that it talks about:

- Gathers enough relevant information to understand specific issues and events
- Uses information to identify problems and draw logical conclusions
- Makes good decisions

2. Look at the **Positive Indicators**. You will see that some of them give you a clue as to what is required:

- Identifies where to get information and gets it

Matching to Core Competencies

- Separates relevant information from irrelevant information
- Identifies and links causes and effects
- Takes a systematic approach to solving problems
- Makes good decisions that take account of all relevant factors

They clearly indicate that you have to gather information to help identify the cause of the problem and then take a systematic approach to solving it.

3. By contrast, if you look at the **Negative Indicators** they will tell you what behaviours you should not exhibit!

4. Now consider the simple problem solving model SARA to give you a structure on which to build the information you have read about in the competency:

> **S**earching - When you perceive you have a problem it is important that you look at it carefully, from all angles, to confirm this is an issue that needs resolving.
>
> **A**nalysing – when you have confirmed there is a problem it is important to analyse it to establish the root causes. You must dig deep into the problem by examining information, documents, speaking to people and looking

Matching to Core Competencies

at the knock-on effects and how it impacts on other systems and processes.

Responding – this is about making an informed decision about what is to be done to resolve the problem and putting in place measures and changes to deal with the issues. The actions you take should deal with the causes of the problem rather than just treating the symptoms.

Assessing – after the measures have been put in place it is important to check that the decisions that have been made to deal with the issues were effective. Follow up checks must be made to ensure the causes of the problem have been eliminated.

You should now be in a position where you understand what is required and all you have to do is think of an occasion when you solved a problem in this way. Once you have the example, break it down into the elements they are looking for in the description of the competency.

If you are still finding this difficult, a good tip is to make sure you avoid dismissing an example because you feel it does not seem dynamic or glamorous enough. Sometimes it is the simple examples which are the best and can be structured for a very effective delivery. Also, talk to friends and colleagues to help you identify examples.

By the time you have matched yourself to all the competencies you will have an understanding of each one and be confident you have discovered your strengths and areas for development. The matching process is the first step in preparing yourself for completion of the application form and attending the selection board.

Behavioural Assessment

One of the tools used to assess competencies is the ***Behavioural Assessment*** model. The premise behind behavioural assessment is that the most accurate predictor of future performance is past performance in a similar situation. Structured assessment, whether of written applications or personal interviews, focus on experiences, behaviours, knowledge, skills and abilities that are job related. Keep in mind that the assessor is usually evaluating you against the profile of desired behaviours considered necessary for that role or rank.

When preparing your written or verbal scenarios give specific and detailed responses in which you describe a particular situation that relates to the question. Briefly describe the situation, what you did and the result or outcome. A complete answer should contain four elements: Situation,

Task (Objective), Action and Result. This is the STAR methodology.

Situation:
> Set the stage for the assessor by providing an overview of the situation and any relevant background information. Be specific and succinct.

Task/Objective:
> What were you trying to achieve or what goal(s) were you working toward?

Action:
> Describe the actions you took to address the situation with an appropriate amount of detail. What specific steps did you take and how did you go about it?

Result:
> Describe the outcome of your actions and do not be shy about taking credit for your behaviour. Your answer should contain multiple positive results whenever possible.

The assessor or interviewer wants to know what you did. The operative word is 'I', not 'we' (unless it is team working and 'we' will be appropriate for some parts of your example).

Focus on providing specifics and avoid generalities, opinions, or future oriented statements. Your answer can have a negative result or outcome if you explain what you learned or would do differently in the future.

STAR Example

The example that follows is an applicant for promotion to sergeant. It demonstrates how the STAR methodology can be used to assist in putting together a well structured competency based answer and how it might be marked by the force. The example is an answer to the resilience competency.

Background

In this case the applicant is a female constable with six years service. She was originally part of a section of six constables consisting of two probationary constables; one at the start and one at the end of their probationary periods. Two other officers have 5 and 27 years service respectively. The shift sergeant is currently absent on an extended period of sick leave.

The applicant was appointed as acting sergeant in charge of the five remaining constables. The section was regarded as poor performing due to a low work rate and lack of team cohesion. The local superintendent had focused on the poor performance and required significant improvement. The applicant was tasked with turning performance around.

Application Form

The completion of the application form was subject to strict rules for submission, including a time scale for delivery to force headquarters. The application was supported by the Divisional Commander, a mandatory requirement of force policy. The Resilience question was:

'Provide a recent example of how you have demonstrated resilience in the work place, to the required level, for the rank of sergeant'.

The applicant, who had received prior training in the use of the STAR methodology, provided the following written example:

Situation.
Appointed acting sergeant with the remit to improve overall performance.

Task/Objective.
To improve shift performance, cohesiveness and morale within three months.

Action.
I addressed the team articulating my vision for the immediate future. I spoke to each section member, assessed their skills, experience and development needs. I reviewed individual workloads and completed PDR 'SMART' professional and development objectives. I also set team objectives. PC 'A' refused to agree to the performance plan. I firmly pointed the consequences of failing to comply and why it was required to

Matching to Core Competencies

> *comply with the divisional and force plan. I held weekly personal reviews and team meetings to discuss performance. I coached officers on an individual basis and dealt with personal issues. I worked in my own time to ensure project was completed. I lobbied the superintendent to recognise good work.*
>
> **Result**.
> *Individual and team performance improved. Officers achieved individual objectives and team targets were met. Resistance disappeared through satisfaction and pride at the achievements. The superintendent congratulated the section at briefing for the good work and two team members received formal letters of congratulation. The superintendent congratulated me saying, '...you displayed high levels of reliability and resilience in very unusual circumstances. Performed well, delivering a demanding action plan'.*
>
> (200 words)

The Resilience competency for the rank of Sergeant is shown below. Note the **required level**, the **positive indicators** and **negative indicators** which are used to mark the answer.

RESILIENCE	Shows resilience, even in difficult circumstances. Prepared to make difficult decisions and has the confidence to see them through.
Required Level	Shows reliability and resilience in difficult circumstances. Remains calm and confident, and responds logically and decisively in difficult situations
Positive Indicators	

- Is reliable in a crisis, remains calm and thinks clearly.
- Sorts out conflict and deals with hostility and provocation in a calm and restrained way.
- Responds to challenges rationally, avoids inappropriate emotion.
- Deals with difficult emotional issues and then moves on.
- Manages conflicting pressures and tensions.

Matching to Core Competencies

- Maintains professional ethics when confronted with pressure from others.
- Copes with ambiguity; deals with uncertainty and frustration.
- Resists pressure to make quick decisions where full consideration is needed.
- Remains focused and in control of situations.
- Makes and carries through decisions, even if they are unpopular, difficult or controversial.
- Stands firmly by a position when it is right to do so.
- Deals confidently with members of the public, drawing on own skills and experience.
- Is comfortable working alone with an appropriate level of supervision and guidance.
- Puts a positive view on situations and concentrates on what can be achieved.
- Is aware of and manages personal stress.
- Accepts criticism and praise.
- Does not get emotionally involved in disputes.
- Is patient when dealing with people who make complaints.
- Acts in a confident way when challenged.
- Says 'no' when necessary.

Negative Indicators

- Gets easily upset, frustrated and annoyed.
- Panics and becomes agitated when problems arise.
- Walks away from confrontation when it would be more appropriate to get involved.
- Needs constant reassurance, support and supervision.
- Uses inappropriate physical force.
- Gets too emotionally involved in situations.
- Reacts inappropriately when faced with rude or abusive people.
- Deals with situations aggressively.
- Complains and whines about problems rather than dealing with them.
- Gives in inappropriately when under pressure.
- Worries about making mistakes, avoids difficult situations.

Headquarters Assessment Panel

The panel is responsible for assessing applications and short listing candidates for interview. It can consist of two or three trained assessors and it is common practice for the Police Federation to be involved. There will be a structured marking guide designed to fairly and consistently assess the application answers.

Police forces tend to design their own marking guides to meet local needs. What follows is an example of one approach to marking the application answer:

Assessment panel – Marking Criteria

1) Did the candidate comply with the instructions for submission? Yes/No*

   (*If 'no' candidate is **failed** at this point. Reasons to be clearly stated.)

2) Does the candidate provide a brief and logical overview of the example? Yes/No.

3) Does the candidate establish the purpose for the example? Yes/No.

4) Does the candidate, clearly identify the action that was considered, planned and executed as part of this example? Yes/No.

5) Are the results and conclusions achieved, consistent with the activity, ethics and original purpose of the example? Yes/No.

Resilience – The required level

'Shows reliability and resilience in difficult circumstances. Remains calm and confident, and responds logically and decisively in difficult situations'

Does the candidate demonstrate the positive indicators, if relevant, in the example?

- Is reliable in a crisis, remains clam and thinks clearly

  …Remained calm, set personal and team objectives and targets. Supt's comments noted.

- Sorts out conflict and deals with hostility and provocation in a calm and restrained way

  …Officers were left in no doubt where things were going.

- Responds to challenges rationally, avoids inappropriate emotion

  …PC 'A' informed why it was required and made clear of consequences of not doing it.

- Deals with difficult emotional issues and then moves on

  …Not directly evidenced.

- Manages conflicting pressures and tensions.

  …Worked alone. Under pressure from Supt. and section – strong area.

Matching to Core Competencies

- Maintains professional ethics when confronted with pressure from others

    ...Evidenced from challenge by PC 'A'

- Copes with ambiguity; deals with uncertainty and frustration

    ...Dealt with uncertainty and frustration of officers on section. Results demonstrate a change of attitude on section.

- Resists pressure to make quick decision where full consideration is needed

    ...Put together a 3 month plan. Resisted the impulse to get quick results although under pressure to get results. Good area.

- Remains focused and in control of situations

    ...Evidence of focus on task and control through weekly personal reviews and team meetings.

- Makes and carries through decisions, even if unpopular, difficult or controversial

    ...Unpopularity evidenced. Officers resisted and one challenged. Saw the project through to success.

- Stands firmly by a position when right to do so

    ...Stood firm. Supported Divisional and Force Policing Plan.

- Deals confidently with members of the public, drawing on own skills and experience.

    ...Not evidenced. Internal issue.

Matching to Core Competencies

- Is comfortable working alone with an appropriate level of supervision and guidance

    ...Evidence suggests can work alone and see things through.

- Puts a positive view on situations and concentrates on what can be achieved

    ...Conscious of raising morale and team cohesiveness and resisting impulse to get a quick fix.

- Is aware of and manages personal stress

    ...Coached officers and dealt with personal issues. Also, worked in own time.

- Accepts criticism and praise

    ...No evidence of criticism but received compliment from superintendent.

- Does not get emotionally involved in disputes

    ...Not directly evidenced but appears to have demonstrated the appropriate level of emotional involvement e.g. aware of officers personal issues.

- Is patient when dealing with people who make complaints

    ...Dealt with officer who disagreed and explained the significance of the plan and the consequences of non-compliance.

- Acts in a confident way when challenged

> ...Overall, the evidence implies that there was a high degree of confidence and the challenges were dealt with firmly with positive outcomes.

- Says 'no' when necessary

> ...Not evidenced but demonstrated clear determination to see the project through and resisted other contrary views.

Negative Indicators

Does the candidate include any negative indicators?

Yes/No

Evidence……………………………………………………….

Decision of the Panel

Does the candidate reach the required standard for the core competency of Resilience?

A = Passed with clear evidence. Is above the required level.
B = Passed with evidence at the required level.

C = Failed to reach the required level.

D = Failed to reach the required level. Little or no evidence offered.

Matching to Core Competencies

Summary

This example demonstrates a typical marking guide. Forces have different approaches but there is commonality through structured and evidenced processes. To ensure you can prepare a high quality application you should obtain as much information about the process as possible. Some Forces hold briefing sessions to disseminate information about the process.

In addition to understanding and using the STAR approach, there are some important issues for you as you contemplate before submitting an application. These include:

1) Are you qualified? Not just by the relevant 'OSPRE' examinations, but the other qualifying criteria that your force may have applied to the application?
2) Do I have any relevant complaints or misconduct issues that may bar my progress at this time?
3) Can I present sufficient good quality evidence for any question I am required to answer?
4) Is that evidence to the required level for all competencies tested?

If you are honest with yourself and carry out this simple audit you will avoid disappointment further on in the process. There is nothing worse than building up your expectations and then having them dashed by something you have overlooked. If you can eliminate any stumbling blocks you can go forward with confidence.

Personal Development Assessment

Consider what you have learned in this chapter about matching to core competencies and make an assessment of your developmental needs. This will help you to identify and collate, chapter by chapter, areas you need to consider for inclusion in your Personal Action Plan.

1. What **gaps** in your knowledge do you have on matching to core competencies?

2. What **actions** can you take in the work place or elsewhere to improve knowledge of your matching to core competencies?

3. How do you rate your **skills** in this area?

Rate yourself with a score out of 10.
(10 high, 1 low)

10

Chapter 7

Matching to Strategy

Aims

This chapter will introduce you to the fundamental elements of matching to strategy and enable you to:

- **Describe strategy**

- **Describe situational vision and leadership**

- **Describe how to match yourself to strategy**

- **Assess your current strategic development needs**

Introduction

Strategy can make people glaze over with confusion or boredom. Unfortunately, by reputation, it is perceived to be full of 'management speak' and alien to the work environment. In fact, the general perception of the work force is that strategy is of interest to senior management and those who are seeking promotion.

This perception is often reinforced by the apparent lack of impact that strategy has on the work of the patrolling officer. It often seems unrelated to daily response work.

Herein lies the challenge for a situational manager. If they are to translate the organisational vision into actions for teams and individuals to accomplish, then a thorough understanding of the theoretical basis to strategy is required. Unraveling the strategic maze is the first step.

Understanding Strategy

To understand strategy it is essential to be clear about the words and language used by strategic planners.

Strategic Decisions – These are the decisions taken by the senior management team that determine the overall direction of the organisation to meet the demands and requirements. This is often characterised an aim or mission statement.

Strategy – This is the pattern or plan that pulls together the major goals into a cohesive structure that supports the achievement of the aim or mission of the organisation.

Objectives – These state what is to be achieved and when results have to be accomplished.

Tactics – These are the step by step sequences of actions defining how the objectives are to be achieved. These are characterised by the familiar SMART approach – Specific, Measurable, Achievable, Realistic and Timed - to achieving objectives. Structured approaches to managing the tactical delivery of projects to deliver on the Strategic Plan are common place and come under the banner Programme Management.

Policies – These determine the rules or guidelines that express the limits within which the tactics can be pursued. Frequently, these will be about financial limits, time frames and resource limitations.

Matching to Strategy

STRATEGIC DECISIONS	➡	Decisions that determine the OVERALL DIRECTION of the organisation in response to demands
STRATEGY	➡	PATTERN OR PLAN That integrates an organisations major goals into a cohesive whole
OBJECTIVES	➡	State WHAT is to be achieved & when WHEN results are to be accomplished
TACTICS	➡	Step by step sequence of actions defining HOW We achieve objectives
POLICIES	➡	RULES OR GUIDE LINES that express THE LIMITS within which tactics should occur

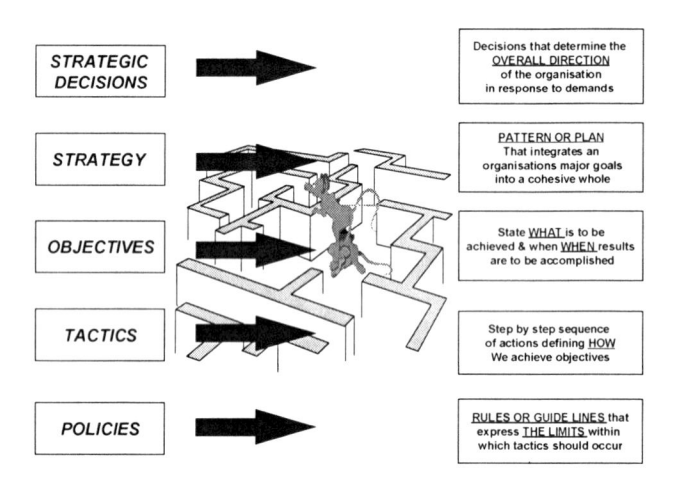

Strategy in Action

The aim/mission and values of an organisation represent the **Strategic Decisions.** This is the vision or overall direction and states what is intended to be achieved. A vision must be supported by a solid **Strategy** otherwise the vision will be nothing more than a dream. The strategy will be broad key themes or activities that directly support the vision like *'Helping the Public'* or *'Reducing Crime'.*

Matching to Strategy

A typical example:

```
   ┌──────────┐         ┌──────────┐
   │ Reducing │         │Investigating│
   │  Crime   │         │   Crime   │
   └──────────┘   ╱‾‾╲  └──────────┘
              ( Aim/Mission )
   ┌──────────┐   ╲__╱  ┌──────────┐
   │Promoting │         │          │
   │Safety and│         │ Helping  │
   │ Security │         │The Public│
   └──────────┘         └──────────┘
```

Falling out of each of the supporting pillars of the strategy will be key ***Objectives*** that are designed to achieve results in that particular area of activity. For example, under the key pillar Reducing Crime there will be a number of objectives designed to drive crime down.

Matching to Strategy

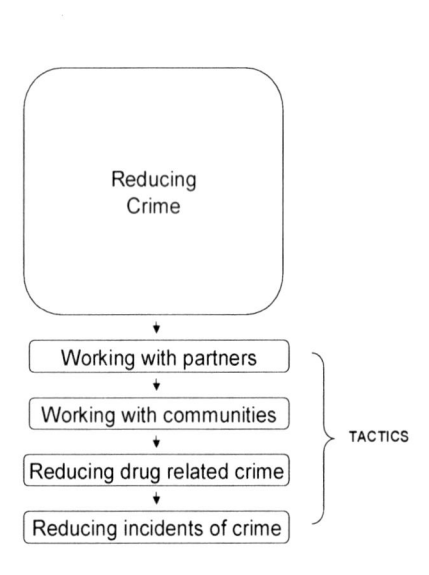

```
            ┌─────────────┐
            │             │
            │  Reducing   │
            │   Crime     │
            │             │
            └──────┬──────┘
                   ↓
        ┌──────────────────────┐  ⎫
        │ Working with partners│  ⎪
        └──────────┬───────────┘  ⎪
                   ↓              ⎪
        ┌──────────────────────┐  ⎪
        │Working with communities│ ⎬  TACTICS
        └──────────┬───────────┘  ⎪
                   ↓              ⎪
        ┌──────────────────────┐  ⎪
        │Reducing drug related crime│ ⎪
        └──────────┬───────────┘  ⎪
                   ↓              ⎪
        ┌──────────────────────┐  ⎪
        │Reducing incidents of crime│ ⎭
        └──────────────────────┘
```

Each of the objectives will be managed as a separate project as described above and the actions that are taken to achieve each objective are the **Tactics**.

Matching to Strategy

Situational Vision

As we know from Chapter 5 on management skills the role of the manager is to understand the strategic direction of the organisation and be able to translate it into a situational vision where employees are given tactical actions that directly support the vision of the organisation.

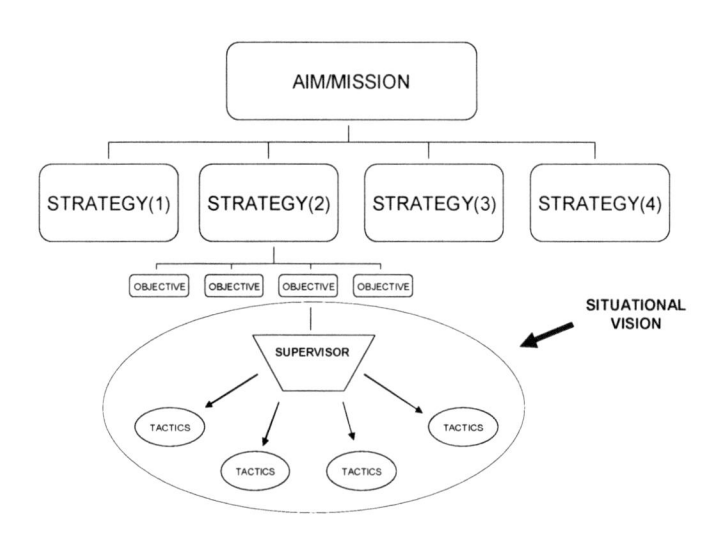

```
                        AIM/MISSION
          ┌──────────────┬┴─────────────┬──────────────┐
     STRATEGY(1)    STRATEGY(2)    STRATEGY(3)    STRATEGY(4)
                         │
              ┌────┬─────┼─────┬────┐
          OBJECTIVE OBJECTIVE OBJECTIVE OBJECTIVE
                         │
                     SUPERVISOR              ← SITUATIONAL VISION
              ↙    ↙    ↓    ↘
          TACTICS TACTICS TACTICS TACTICS
```

It is, therefore, important to understand the aim/mission, values and the strategic plan of the organisation. Understanding what is required will enable supervisors and managers to effectively direct how the work will be done to achieve it.

Matching to Strategy

Understanding the strategy of the organisation in which you hope to be selected is fundamental to your success. It is important to know that you match the core competencies required of the role as described in chapter 6 but, in the same way, it is equally important to understand what the organisation stands for and what kind of people they are looking for to achieve the stated aims.

Just as we recognise that policing is a diverse occupation comprising an eclectic group of people with different styles and interests, we must recognise that chief officers have different approaches to policing. Zero tolerance, community based policing, traffic matters, drug rehabilitation vs. enforcement and controversial methods of dealing with offenders like Restorative Justice are all different approaches that have characterised different chief officers and moulded policing strategies.

In addition, the strategy and style of policing will be influenced by the nature of the policing environment. For example, policing the railways, Ministry of Defence establishments, rural areas and metropolitan districts all require different styles of policing.

Whatever the style of policing is in a particular force it is essential to examine the policing plan to determine the vision of the force and the type of people they want in the organisation. When you know what they are looking for you can determine how your personality fits the model.

A quick look at the aim/mission and values can tell you a lot about the organisation.

For example:

Metropolitan Police (2006)

Our Mission

- *Working together for a safer London*

Our Values

- *We will have pride in delivering quality policing. There is no greater priority*
- *We will build trust by listening and responding*
- *We will respect and support each other and work as a team*
- *We will learn from experience and find ways to be even better*
- *We are one team – we all have a duty to play our part in making London safer*

In this example there is a strong emphasis on working together, safety, quality policing,

Matching to Strategy

building trust, learning from experience and team working.

Thames Valley Police (2006)

Our Aim

Working with communities to reduce crime, disorder and the fear of crime as a leading, caring and professional police service.

Our Values

We are people of integrity who:

- *Listen and learn*
- *Work together and do what we say we are going to do*
- *Take responsibility for solving problems*
- *Earn trust and respect*
- *Are courageous, open and fair to all*
- *Challenge, innovate and achieve*
- *Hold ourselves and others accountable for performance.*

In this example there is strong emphasis on working with communities, reducing crime, disorder, fear, accountability, listening, learning, problem solving, responsibility, trust, courage and innovation.

When you know what the force stands for and the type of people they are looking for, all you

Matching to Strategy

have to do is identify where your personality matches. If it does not, then you need to analyse where you are and develop your personality to fit the model required.

The next step is to take a close look at how the force intends to achieve its aim/mission by examining the main strands of the strategy. So, for example, if one of the main pillars supporting the aim/mission is Reducing Crime, as in the example given above, then you must understand what objectives are being pursued to achieve an outcome and examine them closely to understand how they are to be achieved.

For example, if one of the objectives is to 'Reduce Drug Related Crime', what is the force approach to achieving an outcome?

1. Is it to focus on education? If so, how is it intended to do that?
2. Is it enforcement? If so, how are they intending to do that?
3. Is it treatment? If so how are they intending to do that?

Examining each of these issues will give you a clear picture of the way in which it is intended to make the strategy successful. If you believe this is the best way of dealing with these issues you match the belief systems of the organisation. In consequence, you will be able to support the direction the force is going. Team leaders will be able to develop a situational vision to create appropriate tactical actions and individuals will be able to manage their daily work in line with the force aim/mission.

On the other hand, if you do not believe in the strategy it will become a self-fulfilling philosophy and you will not match. If you go to an interview with that in mind, it is unlikely that the interview panel will be convinced you are the person they want in their organisation.

Strategic Perspective Competency

Strategic Perspective does not appear in the competencies for constables or sergeants. This does not mean that it is irrelevant for those ranks. To the contrary, if you demonstrate a good knowledge of what the force stands for, the direction it is going and where you fit in, the more likely you are to impress a selection board and demonstrate that you have future potential beyond your immediate target role or rank.

It does, however, appear in the competencies for inspector and above and an increasing emphasis is placed on the skills that individuals possess in this area. It is important to develop and select leaders who are transformational and take a broader view of what the organisation is trying to achieve. They need to understand the key issues that support the force strategy and how it all fits together to achieve the organisational goals. In addition, it is important to take a broader view of force strategy and understand where it fits with the interests and aims of other units inside and outside the organisation. Also, there is a requirement to think ahead to identify key issues and prepare for future challenges.

This begins to sound like they are looking for strategists! To an extent that is true. It is fundamental that you should understand what strategy is and be able to articulate it. However, the key to this is being able to translate the strategy into action. This is the situational vision mentioned above. It is likely that any selection board will want to probe this area to test whether the skills are present because that is what the force wants; people who understand the direction the force is going and who can focus daily activities on achieving the force aims.

The positive indicators in the strategic perspective competency are very explicit about what is required. They are focused on four main areas of activity:

1. Situational Leadership

Making sure that their teams methods of working are in line with and concentrate on issues that support the overall strategy of the force.

2. Internal Impact

Thinking strategically beyond their own role and specialist area by understanding how their actions will affect other people who perform different functions and operate in other units.

3. Influencing

Educate people by raising awareness of strategic issues and finding ways of exposing them to ways of working outside the police service. Also, to influence strategy, culture and the general direction of the organisation.

4. Predicting the Future

Has a clear vision of the future by predicting complex problems and issues and taking appropriate action even though there is a need to focus on quick time responses. Also, being able to predict, and prepare for, changes to legislation that will effect the organisation.

Looking through these four areas it is clear that there are elements that overlap with the competencies openness to change and effective communication.

Openness to Change is about recognising and responding to change to improve operational performance by developing new systems, encouraging staff to be flexible, innovative and open to change. Also, actively promoting change through encouraging people to recognise the need for it and managing resistance to it by changing organisational culture.

Effective Communication is about communicating ideas and information effectively, both verbally and in writing, using language and a style of communication that is appropriate to the situation and people being addressed. Also, makes sure that others understand what is going on.

If these three competencies are well evidenced they provide a really solid bedrock for any bid for to be selected for a specialist unit or promotion. So, whatever angle you approach the selection board from, it is advisable to put some effort into preparing these three competencies and recognising where they are mutually supportive.

For information the definition, standard required and positive indicators in the 'Strategic Perspective' competency follow:

Matching to Strategy

Definition

Looks at issues with a broad view to achieve the organisation's goals. Thinks ahead and prepares for the future.

Standard-Level B

Concentrates on issues that support the broad organisational strategy. Maintains a broad view, and understands and considers the interests and aims of other units or outside organisations.

Positive Indicators

- *Makes sure own team's ways of working are in line with the strategic direction of the organisation.*
- *Concentrates on issues that support organisational strategy.*
- *Thinks across functional and unit boundaries, understanding how their actions will affect other people.*
- *Thinks strategically beyond own role or specialist area.*
- *Raises awareness of strategic issues.*
- *Finds ways of exposing people to ways of working outside the service.*
- *Tries to influence organisational strategy, culture and direction.*
- *Predicts the effects of complex problems and issues and takes appropriate action.*

- *Considers the longer term and broader view, even when having to respond quickly.*
- *Predicts the effect of legislation on the organisation and prepares for it.*

Summary

Strategy is extremely important to any candidate who intends to get into a specialist department or to be promoted. The key components need to be understood and clearly articulated to demonstrate an understanding of what the organisation is trying to achieve and how it is to be achieved. Individuals in the organisation must know how their area of work contributes to the achievement of the force aim. Team leaders must develop their own situational vision that will focus and guide the work of others.

In addition, it follows that the competencies strategic perspective, openness to change and communication are areas where there will need to be sufficient evidence to convince a panel that you really do believe in the strategy of the organisation and you know how what you do as an individual or team leader matters. It is probably time to consider the force strategy in detail and start living and breathing it.

Matching to Strategy

Personal Development Assessment

Consider what you have learned in this chapter about strategy and make an assessment of your developmental needs. This will help you to identify and collate, chapter by chapter, areas you need to consider for inclusion in your Personal Action Plan.

1. What **gaps** in your knowledge do you have on strategy?

2. What **actions** can you take in the work place or elsewhere to improve knowledge of your strategy?

3. How do you rate your **skills** in this area?

      Rate yourself with a score out of 10.
      (10 high, 1 low)

10

Chapter 8

Diversity

Aims

This chapter will introduce you to the fundamental elements of diversity and enable you to:

- **Describe diversity**

- **Describe the National Learning Requirement**

- **Describe discrimination law**

- **Describe the National Occupational Standards**

- **Assess your current personal development needs**

Introduction

In any application for specialisation or promotion it is essential to recognise that diversity is extremely important. Failure to understand and demonstrate the principles of diversity can be fatal to an application, even if performance in other areas is good. Police officers are expected to represent high standards of integrity and morality in the community because the public expect them to discharge their duties fairly and impartially. In addition, because they are the instruments of strong political will to move towards an integrated and tolerant society, police officers must operate within and promote principles of diversity.

Recent years have seen much greater acceptance of issues that, in the past, were unacceptable to many people. So, issues of sexuality, race, religion, age and disability have been dealt with head-on.

All police staff must have a thorough understanding of all diversity issues and must be able to:

- Understand force strategy on race and diversity
- Recognise and deal with inappropriate words or behaviour
- Translate diversity training and strategy into work place activity

- Recognise and reward good practice
- Recognise and support individuals who have development needs
- Support individual needs analysis and continuous professional development (CPD).

To enable this to happen a broad understanding of the issues in relation to diversity, training, the law and required standards is essential.

McPherson Report 1997

The report by Sir William McPherson QC (1997) into the death of Stephen Lawrence dealt with many of these issues. There were seventy recommendations falling out of the inquiry and one significant finding was that the Metropolitan Police were found to be 'Institutionally Racist'. By definition, this applied to the police service in general.

The report recognised that institutions, like the police service, had grown around accepted society norms and none of these took into account the needs of, for example, a Muslim who wished to pray three times during the working day. The traditional working day may include a refreshment break at 10.30am and 3pm, which is acceptable to those brought up within accepted practices in the UK, but these do not take into account the needs of the Muslim. There was a recognition that society had to change from the established rigid approaches of the past where, wittingly or unwittingly, we excluded minority groups.

Equality vs. Diversity

The position before McPherson was, therefore, one of treating people equally. This was flawed because by applying the same standards to all people we will exclude certain groups. The position now is that we must have a flexible and fair approach. We must do positive things to include everyone and provide opportunities for all by treating everyone fairly and meeting their individual needs.

The Respect for Race and Diversity competency requires you to understand this and to be sensitised to people's needs and beliefs. Diversity is now a broad subject and includes race, religion, cultural beliefs, sexuality, age, disability and size. It also includes personal beliefs on abortion, fox hunting and almost any subject where tolerance and understanding are required. The only caveat on tolerance is criminality. Clearly, criminality cannot be tolerated and it is important to recognise where the boundaries lie.

Police staff must demonstrate understanding of diversity by treating people with respect. They must also show concern for their problems, make them feel valued, understand social customs and challenge attitudes and behaviours that are abusive, aggressive and discriminatory.

The positive indicators of the competency clearly lay out what kind of behaviour should be demonstrated and the negative indicators provide the contrast. For example, negative indicators like 'Using behaviour inappropriately', 'Shows little understanding of the cultural and religious beliefs of different cultures' and 'Does not consider other people's feelings'. It becomes clear what is required for this competency.

Acknowledging how things should be in relation to diversity in the police service, it is worth assessing just how far things have progressed since the McPherson report in 1997.

The Current Position

HMIC – Inspection of Race and Diversity Training 2002

In 2002 Her Majesty's Inspector of Constabulary (HMIC) carried out an inspection of race and diversity training in the police service. This led to the publication of 'Diversity Matters' in April 2003. This report made a number of recommendations about training and the wider understanding of race and diversity issues within the police service.

Diversity

The 'Diversity Matters' Thematic Inspection also highlighted that, in the 20 years since the Scarman Report (1981), none of the key issues discussed by the Police Training Council Working Party (PTCWP) report (1983) had been adequately addressed in training programmes. This finding, combined with the position in 2003, suggested there was considerable urgency to implement effective race and diversity training.

This was further compounded by a BBC television documentary 'The Secret Policeman' (2003) which featured an investigative journalist, Mark Daly, who joined Greater Manchester Police. During his training at a national police training centre in Warrington he made undercover recordings of fellow recruits that exposed prejudice and racist behaviours. Clearly, this raised the whole issue of how far issues of diversity had been addressed by the service, particularly in the area of recruiting.

A key message falling out of 'Diversity Matters' is that the service needs to produce "a clear, well-articulated learning requirement setting out what must be achieved in terms of the desired outcomes". The Inspectorate also found training in race and diversity to be "reasonably efficient in terms of meeting targets, but not totally effective in delivering organisational change".

The main findings were:

Diversity

- The overall strategy for training and development in this area lacks clarity, direction and unified commitment
- The learning requirement is not clearly articulated and it is unclear what outcomes are to be achieved, which has undermined the Specialist Support Unit contract approach
- Training delivery and evaluation is inconsistent and lacks robust quality assurance processes and ownership
- The various staff appraisal systems do not explicitly link with and support the training being delivered
- Ineffective or inadequate supervision/line management undermines any message that is contained within training
- Race and diversity content is not, as suggested, fully integrated into all aspects of police training and development
- The processes of selection, assessment, management and support for trainers delivering race and diversity content are not totally satisfactory
- The training provided to police trainers in respect of race and diversity is not totally adequate
- There is insufficient community involvement in all aspects of the training cycle

Race and Diversity - National Learning Requirement

The findings were addressed in the 2004 report 'Race and Diversity – National Learning Requirement' by ACC Martin Stuart and Dr. Rachel Cragg. The report laid out the learning requirement for police race and diversity training and recommended that each of the areas was addressed directly. Fundamental issues to be addressed included:

- Clarity, direction and unified commitment from all involved
- Consistency in delivery and evaluation. Although specialised qualified teams of diversity trainers are recommended, there must be a race and diversity awareness and competency demonstrated by all trainers
- Integration within both staff appraisal and promotion systems and into all aspects of police training so as to ensure a greater understanding of how race and diversity issues must not be compartmentalised into a discrete package
- Community involvement in all aspects of the training cycle
- The service needs to release itself from the negative notion of avoiding criticism on equality matters and transform itself into one wanting to learn from and work with the community.

Training Approach

The report went on to say it is important that race and diversity training takes the right approach and incorporates the following principles:

1. Generic training needs for the service based on six areas:

- Race (primary focus)
- Gender
- Disability
- Age
- Sexual orientation
- Religion and beliefs

(Race in the broadest sense should include issues around Gypsy, Traveller, immigrant or asylum seeker communities.)

2. Knowledge

The training of police staff must be able to satisfy the basic requirements of the role in 21st century Britain. Knowledge and understanding in each of these areas should incorporate the service's responsibilities under various strands of equality legislation awareness in areas such as the Race Relations (Amendment) Act (RR(A)A) and Disability Discrimination Act (DDA). (legislation is covered later in this chapter)

3. Practical application

The knowledge must be supported by the practical application of the principles. This is not to underplay the importance of any other broader diversity issue. These and other local issues should be addressed in contextual training tailored to meet local needs. The context of the individual's work environment must be clearly understood. For example, an Officer in Taunton in Devon and Cornwall may have a different working context to an officer working in Slough in Thames Valley Police.

4. Links to standards and objectives

It is important that the National Occupational Standards (NOS) are understood by all involved in policing. (The NOS are covered later in this chapter and are laid out at Appendix 1)

5. Behaviours contained in core competencies are incorporated at the required level

(a) Respect for Race and Diversity

- Considers and shows respect for the opinions, circumstances and feelings of colleagues and members of the public, no matter what their race, religion, position, background, circumstances, status or appearance

- Understands other people's views and takes them into account.
- Is tactful and diplomatic when dealing with people, treating them with dignity and respect at all times.
- Understands and is sensitive to social, cultural and racial differences

(b) Community and Customer Focus

- Understands the complexity and effects of policing diverse communities
- Makes sure the organisation relates to people of all ages, backgrounds and views
- Shows a belief that the organisation is responsible to the local community
- Monitors the service delivery to make sure customers needs are met

(c) Effective Communication

- Delivers effective presentations to a wide variety of audiences
- Uses appropriate visual aids and techniques to get the message across and help understanding
- Explains complex issues simply and puts them into context for others
- Considers how different audiences will interpret information
- Checks how effective communication is to the target audience

- Takes every opportunity to reinforce important messages

(d) National Occupational Standards

Elements of race and diversity are explicit in all of the National Occupational Standards.

The Training Framework

Required Training - All Staff

1. Managing Diversity

A generic programme for all staff to be completed as part of induction to the police service. A taught programme followed by portfolio building and assessment in the training environment and in the workplace through the PDR system. In addition, localised training recognising regional differences and understanding of the minority groups in their community.

2. PDR-Based Review

The framework for diversity training is based on a PDR system that requires management and understanding of individual development needs. It is nevertheless important that individuals are given opportunities to update their knowledge and skills at regular intervals.

Required Training – Rank/Grade Specific

1. Entry Level

Probationers Constables learn to act appropriately in responding to human and social diversity in the community in the Police environment.

2. Managerial: Inspector, Sergeant, Police Staff

To develop:

- Knowledge and understanding of the force's race and diversity policies and strategies
- Skills and knowledge required to identify and deal with inappropriate language or behaviour in a supportive way
- Understanding how to translate race and diversity training and policies in to workplace activity
- Skills to enable them to assess an individual's performance in respect of race and diversity, to recognise and reward noteworthy practice on the part of the individuals that they manage and to be able to identify and support additional race and diversity development needs
- To support others in constructing a needs analysis and CPD plan in relation to race and diversity issues.

- Requires mandatory training to ensure sufficient development to enable the management of policing diverse communities.

3. Strategic: BCU Command Team, Chief Officer

To be able to:

- Lead, manage and embrace race and diversity issues and articulate this commitment to all
- Lead by example
- Demonstrate an active understanding of the diversity of the communities which they police and demonstrate support for race and diversity training of others as appropriate to the local area
- Recognise the significance of national and world events in respect of the impact upon community tension (environmental scanning)
- Regularly update knowledge of race and diversity legislation and implement strategies for dissemination
- To initiate strong links with the community and communicate the operational benefits to the force
- Support, recognise and where necessary develop an internal culture of inclusion of all.

Additionally at Chief Officer level:

- Need to visibly demonstrate commitment and leadership in race and diversity issues, must act as a role model or champion and be fully accessible and visible in the community being served.

4. HR Managers

To equip HR managers with the skills and knowledge to enable them to support police employees in achieving diversity training commensurate with their role / rank / grade

National Occupational Standards (NOS)

National Occupational Standards (NOS) define the skills, knowledge, understanding and level of competence expected of individuals to perform key tasks. Together with a defined assessment strategy, developed in parallel with the standards, they allow a clear assessment of competence against nationally agreed standards of performance for all roles and circumstances.

Today, National Occupational Standards are viewed by modern managers as an indispensable tool for managing a highly skilled workforce. They are used widely to support individual and organisational development and quality assurance at all levels. They provide benchmarks of good practice across the UK.

They also form the basis of qualifications, most commonly National Vocational Qualifications (NVQs) and Scottish Vocational Qualifications (SVQs). The Standards are also used in the Integrated Competency Framework (ICF).

National consultation by Skills for Justice with police forces, the Home Office, Association of police Authorities (APA) and community representatives identified 22 units of NOS as the level of performance at which probationary officers need to be operating prior to confirmation. Student officers will be assessed against these 22 units of NOS during their two-year training period.

The Law – Diversity Issues

Discrimination law in this country is made up of different acts and regulations, each outlawing less favourable treatment on a specific ground: gender, race, disability, sexual orientation, religion and age.

(N.B. the legislation that follows is for general information only and does not take into account commencement dates, amendments or courts judgments. Make sure you check the current status of legislation before quoting it).

1. Sex Discrimination Act 1975 (SDA) as amended by the Employment Equality (Sexual Discrimination) Act 2005

The SDA prohibits discrimination on the grounds of:
- Gender
- Pregnancy/maternity leave
- Gender reassignment
- Married/civil partnership status

It is not unlawful to discriminate against unmarried or single people. Pay is covered by the Equal Pay Act 1970. The SDA applies to employment, training and the provision of goods and services although the protection from discrimination on grounds of gender reassignment applies only to employment and training.

2. Race Relations Act 1976 (RRA) as amended by the Race Relations Amendment Act 2000

The RRA prohibits discrimination on the grounds of:
- Colour
- Race
- Nationality
- Ethnic/national origins

Ethnic group means a group that can show a long, shared history, its own cultural tradition, a common language, literature, religion and a common geographical origin. The courts have decided that racial groups include Jews and

Diversity

Sikhs but not Rastafarians and Muslims. Scottish, Welsh, Irish and English people are viewed as separate racial groups. The RRA applies to employment, training and the provision of goods and services.

3. Disability Discrimination Act 1995 (DDA) as amended by the DDA 2005

The DDA provides protection from discrimination on the grounds of disability. It defines a disability as a physical or mental impairment that affects a person's ability to carry out normal day to day activities. The effect has to be substantial, adverse and long term. Unlike the other equality strands it only protects the minority from discrimination and does not protect the able bodied majority. Substantial means more than minor or trivial. An effect is long term if it has lasted for 12 months, is likely to last for 12 months or is likely to last the rest of the person's life.

Discrimination may be justified if it is *related* to the disability rather than the disability itself but the reason must be substantial and material to the particular circumstances.

The employer has a duty to make *reasonable* adjustments if aspects of employment put the disabled employee at a substantial disadvantage in comparison with others who are not disabled.

Diversity

A failure to make a reasonable adjustment cannot be justified.

The legislation applies to employment, training and the provision of goods and services.

4. Employment Equality (Sexual orientation) Regulations 2003

It is unlawful to discriminate against people because of their sexual orientation which includes orientation towards:

- Persons of the same sex
- Persons of the opposite sex
- Persons of both sexes

It includes discrimination on the basis of a perception, assumption or speculation about someone's sexuality, whether rightly or wrongly held. The regulations apply to employment and training.

5. Employment Equality (Religion and belief) Regulations 2003

It is unlawful to discriminate on the grounds of someone's religion or belief in employment or vocational training. This is defined as any religion, religious belief or similar philosophical belief so it does not include political belief. This includes all major religions as well as Druidism, Paganism and Wicca. It is unlawful to discriminate against someone for not holding or subscribing to a specific religious or similar belief. It could therefore include atheism and agnosticism. The regulations also cover perceptions, assumptions or speculations about someone's beliefs. The regulations apply to employment and training.

6. Sex Discrimination (Gender reassignment) Regulations 1999 and the Gender Recognition Act 2005.

The regulations extend the Sex Discrimination Act to provide protection to anyone who intends to undergo, is undergoing, or has undergone gender reassignment, but only as far as employment and training are concerned.

7. Employment Equality (Age) Regulations 2006

It is unlawful to discriminate against someone on the grounds of their age, which includes anyone of any age or of any age group. It covers employment and training.

8. The Equality Act 2006

This Act introduces the new combined Commission for Equality and Human Rights (see www.CEHR.org.uk). It will also include discrimination in the provision of goods and services for religion and belief and sexual orientation regulations.

Types of Discrimination

There are four main types of discrimination:

Direct

This happens when an employer treats an employee less favourably on a prohibited ground. It cannot be justified except in the case of age discrimination if the justification is a legitimate aim and a proportionate means of achieving it.

Indirect

This occurs when an employer imposes an apparently neutral provision, criterion or practice on a group of employees which has the effect of putting persons within the protected group at a particular disadvantage when compared to others. It is not included in the Disability Discrimination Act which has provisions for disability-related discrimination and reasonable adjustment. Indirect discrimination may, sometimes, be justified.

Victimisation

This involves treating employees less favourably because they make or intend to make a complaint about discrimination. It is necessary to show they have been treated less favourably and that it was because they made a complaint or gave evidence or information and that they did this in good faith.

Harassment

An employee is harassed when, on a prohibited ground, a person engages in unwanted conduct which has the purpose or effect of violating his/her dignity or creating an intimidating, hostile, degrading, humiliating or offensive environment for him/her. This would include bullying where it is done on one of the prohibited grounds.

Genuine Occupational Qualifications/Requirements (GOQ/R)

The legislation recognises that there are certain jobs which must be done by a person of a particular race, sex, sexual orientation, religion or belief etc and employers can claim that a post has a GOQ or GOR in very specific circumstances where it is an essential nature of a job or its duties.

Positive Action

Positive action means giving preferential treatment to an individual or group of people to prevent, or compensate for, past disadvantages and that it is a reasonable thing to do. It is not the same as positive discrimination, which involves treating people more favourably on grounds of sex, race etc and is unlawful. Positive action can include targeted advertisements, training and mentoring.

The duty to promote equality

Like other public bodies, the police service has a duty to promote race, disability and gender equality through Equality Schemes. Many forces, like Thames Valley Police, have published one unified Equality Scheme which covers six strands of diversity: race, gender, faith, sexual orientation, age and disability. The scheme includes activities such as conducting diversity impact assessments of policies and procedures, service delivery, access to buildings, communication and employment.

Diversity

Personal Development Assessment

Consider what you have learned in this chapter about diversity and make an assessment of your developmental needs. This will help you to identify and collate, chapter by chapter, areas you need to consider for inclusion in your Personal Action Plan.

1. What **gaps** in your knowledge do you have on diversity?

2. What **actions** can you take in the work place or elsewhere to improve knowledge of diversity?

3. How do you rate your **skills** in this area?

Rate yourself with a score out of 10.
(10 high, 1 low)

10

Chapter 9

Interview Technique

Aims

This chapter will introduce you to the fundamental elements of interview technique and enable you to:

- **Describe interview technique**

- **Describe how to 'set the agenda'**

- **Describe the 'thinking box'**

- **Describe interview behaviours**

- **Assess your current 'interview technique' development needs**

Interview Technique

Introduction

By the time you have been through the process outlined in Chapter 2 of discovering your personality, matching yourself to the competencies and strategy of the organisation you should have a wealth of information about yourself.

All of this information will be a mix of different facets of your personality and what you have to offer whether you are seeking promotion or specialisation.

This information makes up your **_Personality Profile_** and is an introspective view of all your skills and abilities and where they match.

- SUPERVISORY SKILLS
- PROFESSIONAL SKILLS
- TEAM WORKING
- COMPETENCIES
- STRATEGY
- **PERSONALITY PROFILE**
- INTEGRITY
- LEARNING STYLE
- LEADERSHIP
- EMOTIONAL INTELLIGENCE
- SITUATIONAL VISION
- REPORTING STYLE

Interview Technique

Using your Personality Profile

Now you are aware of these things about yourself the trick is knowing how to use this information to best effect. This is about technique.

There is nothing magical about how you should approach the interview panel. It is a matter of going to the interview with a clear picture of what you want to tell them. You should be on a 'mission' of your own and should have formulated a personal strategy.

If you have completed your preparation, you will go the interview with a clear head and on the offensive. There should never be a time when you go to an interview in fear of what might be said or done during the 45 minutes that you are in the room. If you are sitting in the chair in a defensive posture trying to fend off the questions, you are not going to be successful nor are you going to enjoy the experience.

If you imagine for one moment that you enter the interview room and the interviewer asks you the question, **'Why should we select you?** and then tells you that you have 45 minutes to answer the question. How would you feel?

If you do not know where to start, you are not prepared for the interview. However, if you sit back confident in the knowledge that you have much to tell them and you have a well formulated personal strategy for delivering it, you are prepared.

The reality is that the interview panel will have questions that they will want to ask to elicit information about you in different categories. For example, they will want to know about your personal skills, professional skills, general knowledge and your ability to think logically in different situations. Accepting this is the case it is still possible to drive through your strategy and get across to the panel exactly what you want to tell them about why you should be selected. To do this you will need to set the agenda for the interview.

Setting the Agenda

Accepting that you have a good picture of your personality profile, it is a good idea to begin preparing your agenda by using the frequently asked first question designed as an ice breaker to get you going at the start of the interview, 'Tell us a little about yourself?'. It does not matter what they ask you. If you were asked, 'Why should you be selected?' it is really the same answer. In any case, if you have a well prepared agenda you will be nimble enough to deal with the slightly different inflexion in the response to a question.

Consider the question, **'Tell us a little about yourself?'**

It is most important that you structure a short response under three heads:

Past – Where you were born and brought up, what kind of education you received and how successful were you were academically is always a good point to start. Your parents and the type of upbringing you had can be very important. If, for example, if you moved 26 times before you were 18 years of age because your father was in the services, and you lived in various places across the world, could be a point that you can make about your natural resilience for change and dealing with different peoples and cultures. Similarly, if you were brought up in care then your experiences may be important to the personality that you are. You may also wish to mention your early working experiences.

Working Life – There is no sense in repeating your police career record - times, dates and places - because they will already know that. This is your big opportunity to demonstrate what challenges, experiences and development opportunities you have had. This is where **you** set the agenda.

You should mention different situations you have been involved in at different times in your working life and 'throw down the markers'. For example, 'When I was working at 'Blank Town' I had to deal with the building of the new Orbital Road. This really tested my 'team working skills' and, 'When I was working in the city I had to deal with the clash between the two local ethnic groups I had to show real problem solving skills and had to have a community and customer focus'.

The reality is that as you provide career highlights you are throwing down the 'markers' – things which highlight the competencies they are testing you against and your particular style of working. These will be things that you want them to ask you questions about because you can expand on them and it demonstrates graphically how you dealt with the situation. It will also demonstrate the skills required in that particular competency area.

The great thing is that the panel will be keen to explore some of the points that you have made because they are seeking to test those skill areas. This is about bringing the game to them rather than sitting back and them bringing it to you. By doing this you can throw down the markers knowing that they will want to explore them further. Even if the questions are not predictable, you will have a prepared script. It is an insurance policy to keep you on track.

YOUR AGENDA

- Managing & Developing People
- Maximising Potential
- Problem Solving
- Planning & Organising
- Effective Communication
- Community & Customer Focus
- Respect for Race and Diversity
- Resilience

?   ?

This takes some practice but you will find that you will be able to 'snake' your way through the interview moving from one question to another by opening up another avenue of questioning and moving the interview in the direction that you want it to go – '…of course, this situation involving team working was very similar to the time when I had to demonstrate strong leadership at…'

Obviously, the panel members will have certain areas they wish to probe but you may find, because you have an agenda, you will move from one area to another touching on areas they wish to cover. With practice, you can anticipate the direction they want to go. You will know whether you are succeeding when one member hands over to another and states, 'I was going to ask you four questions but you seem to have answered some of those already, so I only have one question to ask'.

Future – To conclude your short agenda setting answer it is important to state where you see you career going over the next 5 and 10 years. It is always good to demonstrate, as you just have, that your career has so far been a progressive development process and you have every intention of moving it forward in the same way.

Answering Questions

After you have 'warm-up' and set your agenda the panel will want to ask you questions. Normally, where there is a panel of two or three interviewers, the questions will be generically grouped and each interviewer will focus on the allocated area. It may be that they will want to ask questions about force strategy, operational knowledge, personal skills, dealing with scenarios, general policing knowledge and headline controversial issues. All of these will be linked to the competencies and will be delivered through 'closed' or 'open' questions.

Closed questions

Definition

There are two definitions that are used to describe closed questions. A common definition is:

> *A closed question can be answered with either a single word or a short phrase.*

Thus 'How old are you?' and 'Where do you live?' are closed questions. A more limiting definition is:

> *A closed question can be answered with either 'yes' or 'no'.*

Thus 'Are you happy?' and 'Is that a cat I can see over there?' are closed questions, whilst 'How are you?' and even 'How old are you?' are not, by this definition, closed. This limited definition is also sometimes called a 'yes or no' question, for obvious reasons.

Using closed questions

Closed questions have the following characteristics:

- They give you facts.
- They are easy to answer.
- They are quick to answer.
- They keep control of the conversation with the questioner.

Open questions

Definition

An open question can be defined as:

An open question is likely to receive a long answer.

Although any question can receive a long answer, open questions deliberately seek longer answers and are the opposite of closed questions.

Using open questions

Open questions have the following characteristics:

- They ask the respondent to think and reflect.
- They will give you opinions and feelings.
- They hand control of the conversation to the respondent.

Open questions begin with what, why, how, or describe.

Responding to open questions can be intimidating, as they seem to hand the baton of control over to the candidate. However, a well-placed open question and plenty of preparation will leave you in control and enable you to develop your agenda. This then gives you the floor to talk about what you want and to draw the panel through intrigue or an incomplete story in the direction you want to go.

Open questions have become more common in recent years and are designed to give the candidate an opportunity to demonstrate the skills they have to offer. Your preparation will have included setting the agenda and in-depth study of different aspects of policing issues. All that is required in this situation is to deliver a well thought out and structured answer.

The 'Thinking Box'

A structured delivery of your answer to any question is extremely important. An interviewer will want to hear an answer that demonstrates you have a good knowledge of the subject, that you have weighed up the arguments and come to a well reasoned conclusion, and personal viewpoint.

The only way to do this is to have carried out the necessary research into the topic and analysed it so that you can understand the positive and negative aspects of the arguments around the subject. A good way of both studying the topic and delivering an answer on the topic is to use a simple structure like the 'Thinking Box'. This will help you to structure your thoughts around the topic supported by evidence. For example, how would you answer the following question?

Interview Technique

'Should Cannabis be legalised?'

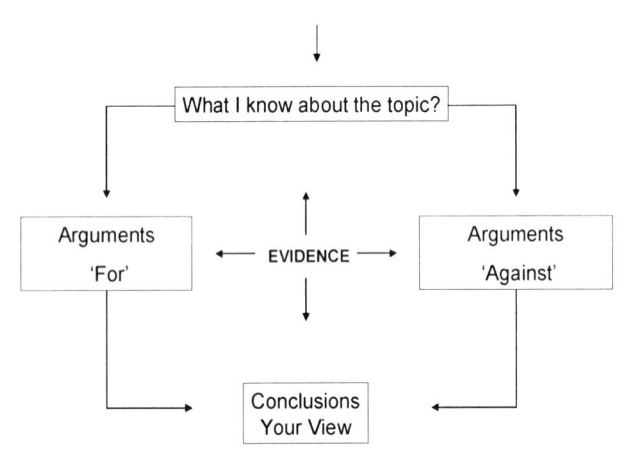

```
                What I know about the topic?
                           │
          ┌────────────────┼────────────────┐
     Arguments    ←── EVIDENCE ──→      Arguments
       'For'                              'Against'
          │                │                │
          └──────────→ Conclusions ←────────┘
                        Your View
```

What do I know about the topic?

- Social consequences of drugs are significant with mental health problems, addiction and death being a feature
- Crime is linked to drug habits and drug supply
- Cannabis is a category C drug
- Alcohol and tobacco are legal drugs and have many social consequences
- Cannabis is supposed to have medicinal properties – being investigated by the Government
- Strategy for tackling drugs is education, enforcement and treatment

Arguments 'Against'

- Legalising will raise the threshold of criminality – the lowest level of criminality will be raised
- More people will take cannabis because it is perceived safe – like alcohol and tobacco
- There will be more health problems - mental illness and death
- More strain on treatment of addicts
- Social impact considerable

Arguments 'For'

- Low level street crime connected with dealers would fade away
- The impure street drugs could be replaced by pure versions which will be safer
- Over the counter sales could fund research into the positive aspects of the drug
- Cannabis cultivation could be a viable commercial enterprise
- People who suffer from medical problems like Multiple Sclerosis (MS) and Arthritis could be given prescription cannabis to alleviate their symptoms

Conclusion/ Your View

In a sense, in questions like these, it does not matter too much what your conclusion and personal view is. Providing it is well reasoned and argued using a structured approach, it will come across as a well considered and thoughtful response to the question.

In this particular topic, you are safe in the knowledge that there are many different viewpoints amongst senior police officers, politicians and other commentators about the best way forward for dealing with cannabis. So far, none of them seems to have produced a solution to the problem.

Now think about topical issues and consider them using the 'Thinking Box' structured approach. For example, routine arming of all police officers, lowering the age of criminal responsibility and lowering the drink driving alcohol limit. This approach to your thought processes will broaden your knowledge of the topic and understanding of the issues.

Interview Behaviours

Researching Panel Members

As an essential part of your preparation it is a good idea to find out who the panel members will be and then research their backgrounds and experience. This will not necessarily give you an indication of the questions you will be asked but it will give you confidence knowing the pedigree of the person to whom you address your answer. In addition, the members of the panel are likely to be impressed if you have done your groundwork and know something about them.

Punctuality

Do make sure you know where the interview will be held. Make sure you know how to get there (by whatever means). If you go by car, you really need to research where you can park. Do not run out of petrol on the way. Leave home earlier than you need to on the day of the interview to deal with delays by traffic or for other reasons. When you get there be courteous to everyone you meet especially the Personal Assistant (PA) or Secretary receiving candidates.

Dress

You should obviously find out what the dress code will be for the interview – whether uniform or civilian clothes. You should dress smartly making special effort to make a good impression. Shoes should be shiny and hair well groomed. If the dress is civilian clothing men should wear a suit and tie. Women should wear a trouser suit with a high neck line. In both cases jewellery should be minimal. Do not wear anything new. Wear something that you are

Interview Technique

familiar with and you will find comfortable sitting in the interview for 45 minutes. Medals are not usually worn with uniform.

Hand Shaking

When you enter the interview room, never announce who you are and then move down the panel vigorously shaking their hands saying how nice it is to meet them and it is a pity the weather is so bad.

Remember, they know who you are and you should take your lead from the Chair of the panel. Wait to be invited to sit down and only shake hands if invited to do so by being offered a hand. If you are offered a handshake use a single hand and it should always be with an open, relaxed palm.

If hand shaking is not part of your culture explain to the panel why you cannot shake hands. They will understand and respect your needs.

Sitting

When you are being interviewed, it is very important that you give out the right signals. You should always look attentive - so do not slouch in your chair. It is a good idea to sit into the back of the chair and consciously feel the chair running up your spine. This will prevent any tendency to lean forward. Keeping your head up will also help. If the chair has arms rest your elbows on them. Whatever you do make sure that you do not lean forward and be tempted to adopt the fetal position and end up looking at the panel from the level of the chair seat!

Hands

These are always a nuisance in formal interview situations because you never know where to put them. You should never fold your arms, nor should you sit on your hands. Most of us use our hands to assist with verbal communication so it is probably best to place your hands in front of you, palms down on your thighs and use them where you feel the need and return to that position. Entwining your fingers and breaking the knuckles and other nervous disorders should be avoided at all costs as they distract the interviewer and it may detract from the quality of your answers.

Legs

Like your hands, these are always a difficult item. You should never cross your legs as this can lead to slipping forward out of the chair and before you know it, you will be in the slouch position and have to pull yourself into the upright position. This is distracting. Also, do not cross your feet out in front of you or tuck them

Interview Technique

under the chair. This can lead to restricted blood flow and your legs or feet may become numb and lead to discomfort or, as a candidate once did, as he stood up to leave his leg collapsed and found himself looking up embarrassingly from the prone position on the floor.

Eye Contact

Always give the panel member that is asking you a question eye contact. This will help you to listen to the question and concentrate on what is being asked of you. Eye contact should not be slavish to the point that you stare at the panel.

It is always good to divert your eyes from direct contact as you think about the delivery of your answer after the question has been asked. Diverting your eyes slightly to the side or above the questioner enables you to maintain contact with the person and think clearly without feeling the pressure of the panel member is on you constantly.

Do not be tempted to look down at the floor, over your right shoulder or out of the window and watch the maintenance woman mowing the grass at the front of Headquarters. This will distract you and create the impression you are unprepared and desperately looking for inspiration.

As you answer a question you should not focus your eye contact solely on the questioner. Your eyes should look to the left and right to make contact with the other panel members. Make them feel that you are addressing the whole panel with your answer.

Also, never turn your back on panel members by shuffling around in the chair to face the questioner. It might make you feel less vulnerable but by obstructing their view of your torso they are less likely to trust you. This is a tribal thing. If you can see someone's head and torso, you can see the most vulnerable areas. This makes you want to trust them

Lying

Never lie to anyone in an interview, your body language and tone of voice or the words you use will probably give you away - classic body language giveaways include scratching your nose and not looking directly at the panel member when you are speaking to them.

Creating the right impression

It is important to create the right impression through facial expression. Smiles, non-verbal communication for listening and appropriate nodding for agreement and understanding are very important. The advice given in this section deals with how to create that perfect corporate face and posture to make the interviewer feel at ease in your presence.

What follows is advice from an actor, Marlowe, who posted a thread on the BBC web site conversation forum for interview techniques. It captures the essence of the issues discussed in this chapter and how you might create the right impression.

The Face – Advice from an actor

"First, and most important of all, preparation. Before your interview, try to visualise yourself as your prospective employers will see you. This isn't easy, but be honest with yourself. If you're ugly as sin, admit it. It makes a difference, like it or not. Now, you need to practise doing The Face. I give it capital letters because it's very, very important, and because I have a healthily over-inflated sense of my own importance.

Stand in front of a mirror and look yourself in the eye. Strike an expression that you would describe as neutral. Don't think too much about this, just do it. Now turn your mouth up at the corners just a little bit. Raise your eyebrows a fraction. Open your eyes just a little wider. Lift your chin up, and be sure that your head is straight and in line with your spine. If you're one of the 30% or so of people who's bottom lip protrudes a few millimetres further than your top lip, make an active effort to pull it back - a jutting lower lip suggests an aggressive and unreasoning nature and a low IQ (think Neanderthal, and you'll see where I'm coming from. Cruel, but true). Okay. Done all that? Good. Hold it. This is the natural expression that your face should fall into during your interview. Your shoulders should be back and your legs should not be too far apart (for a man) or crossed lightly (for a woman).

Now that you've got into this position, what I'm about to tell you next won't make much sense: relax. Even though holding your face like this may feel alien and unnatural, you must give the impression that this is how you approach life each day. If you look constipated, all our hard work was for nothing. You really need to practise this expression until it comes naturally. It's a great tool to have in everyday life as well as in an interview situation. Try it out - you'll be surprised how quickly it will put most people at their ease.

Remember to hold eye contact for a fraction of a second longer than feels comfortable - don't stare, but don't feel as if you have to apologise for looking at someone. If you're English, this will probably be a tremendous problem. We're naturally submissive people who feel that we're probably at error in any given social situation. Again, cruel but true.

Interview Technique

During the interview itself, try to be natural. Don't use the time the interviewer is talking to you to prepare your next answer - if you haven't been listening attentively, it will be blindingly obvious. Punctuate any long speeches by your interviewer with very slight nods of the head - particularly the 'let me tell you a little about what we do here ...' speech. The interviewer knows this by heart, and so is far more interested in your reaction to it. If you are being interviewed by more than one person, switch your attention periodically. It's good practice to address your remarks to one interviewer only if he or she has just asked you a direct question, but don't turn your back on the rest, or obstruct their view of your torso. Apparently this is a tribal thing. If you can see someone's head and torso, you can see the most vulnerable areas. This makes you want to trust them. Good, eh? That's why your handshake should always be with an open, relaxed palm."

Do's and Don'ts

- Don't leave your mobile phone switched on.
- Don't chew gum.
- Try to avoid saying 'um' and 'er...'
- Do try to use correct grammar.
- Don't swear.
- Don't use slang.
- Don't smell of smoke, alcohol or strong deodorant.

Practice, Practice, Practice

Performing well in interviews is just like writing a good Curriculum Vitae (CV) and covering letter - the more practice you get the better you will be. In addition, the more feedback you ask for, the more you can work on your technique in a constructive manner.

Appeals

Normally, forces will have an appeals process in place for selection boards. If a candidate feels they have been unfairly treated by a defect in the process they may be able to appeal. However, it is important to recognise the distinction between process and your performance on the board.

In the former there may be grounds for appeal if the board refused to interview you because you had not supplied the last three performance development reviews; if that was a requirement of the process. The question of whether you did or did not supply them may be subject of an appeal. On the other hand, if you are unhappy that your performance was not correctly assessed, it is less likely that you will have grounds for appeal. You must remember that all decisions about competencies assessed at the application and interview stage are evidenced, normally by a panel. It is obviously much more difficult to make a case in these circumstances

Interview Technique

because the panel will have agreed on the evidence you provided.

If you feel aggrieved by the decision of a selection board, try and remain calm. If you feel that there was a defect in the process follow the appeals process. If you feel that you were not assessed properly it is no good firing off nasty e-mails to the federation and a hard pressed HR department. You will not endear yourself to them and likely give yourself a negative profile. The answer is to seek feed back so that you can understand why you did not perform well or where you specifically went wrong. Build what you learn into your development plan and work on it. Negative attitudes and cynicism are not conducive to success. Remember what was said in Chapter 1 about the different reasons why people fail selection boards.

Interview Technique

Personal Development Assessment

Consider what you have learned in this chapter about interview technique and make an assessment of your developmental needs. This will help you to identify and collate, chapter by chapter, areas you need to consider for inclusion in your Personal Action Plan.

1. What **gaps** in your knowledge do you have on interview techniques?

2. What **actions** can you take in the work place or elsewhere to improve knowledge of interview techniques?

3. How do you rate your **skills** in this area?

Rate yourself with a score out of 10.
(10 high, 1 low)

10

Chapter 10

Personal Action Planning

Aims

This chapter will introduce you to the fundamental elements of personal action planning and enable you to:

- **Review your Personal Development Assessment ratings in each chapter and plot them graphically to prioritise key areas of personal development.**

- **Complete an Activity Plan to highlight ideas for development.**

- **Prepare a Development Plan using SMART objectives.**

- **Identify what help and support you can get from a coach or mentor.**

- **Understand what to expect of a coach or mentor.**

- **Understand experiential learning.**

Introduction

The Personal Development Assessments that you have been compiling at the end of each chapter have provided an opportunity to assess your skills in each of the subject areas.

You will now be able to use this information to create a spider graph visual representation of your skills. This visual image more easily enables you to highlight areas of strength and identify issues on which you can focus development.

Spider Graph

The Personal Development spider graph follows. Just follow the instructions to complete the graph of your skills.

- Identify your score for each Personal Development Assessment at the end of Chapters 2-11.

- Plot each score against the matching skill area on the spider graph.
  NB: the outside circumference represents 10 and centre represents 0.

- When complete, draw a line to connect each plotted dot.

Personal Action Planning

Spider Graph

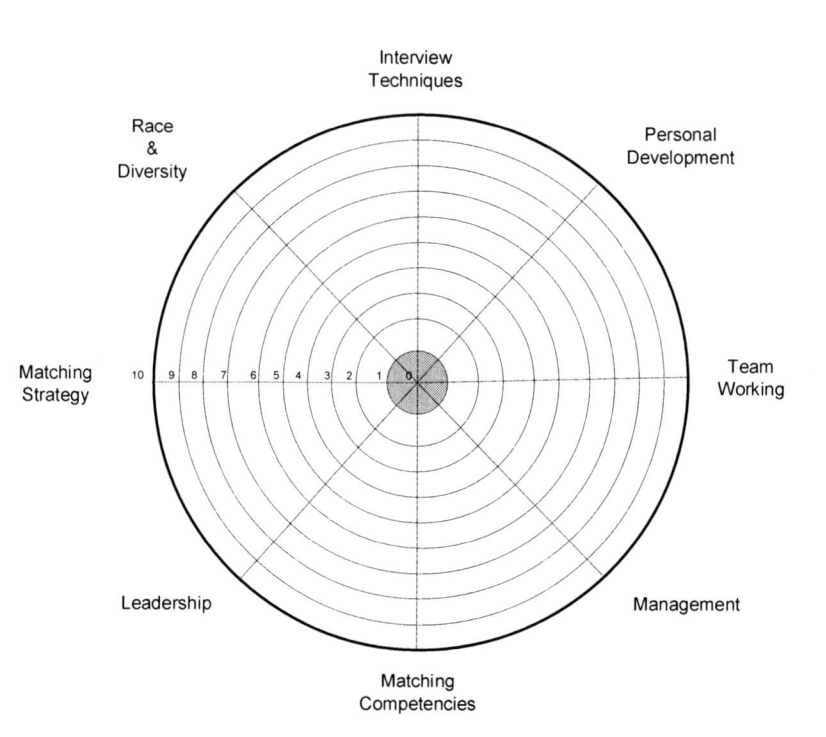

(Spider/radar chart with axes labeled: Interview Techniques, Personal Development, Team Working, Management, Matching Competencies, Leadership, Matching Strategy, Race & Diversity; scale 0–10)

You should now have developed a spider web graph. It will look similar to the graph that follows:

Personal Action Planning

Spider Graph

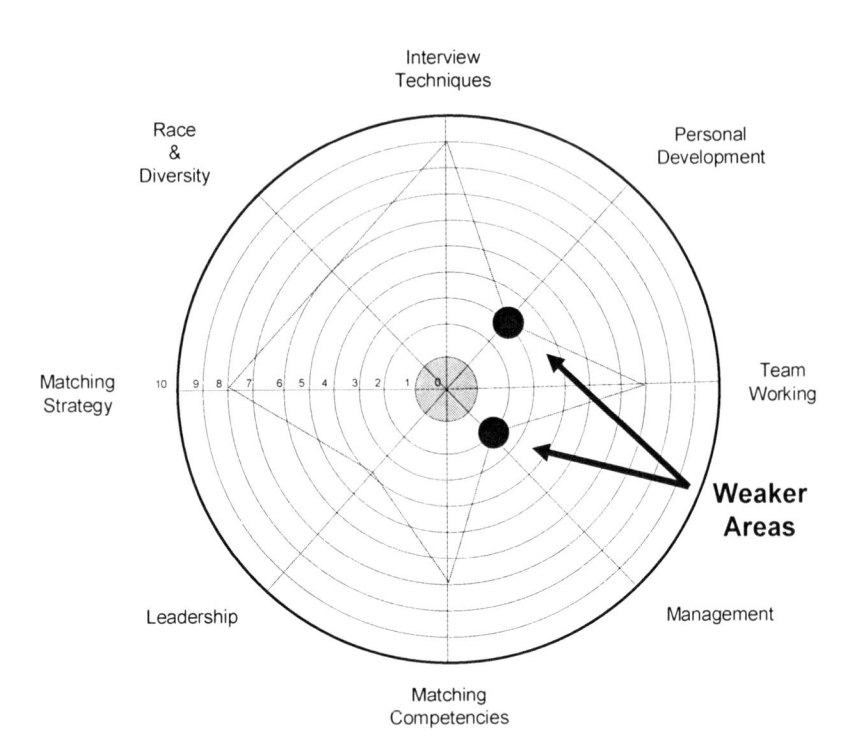

Spider graph with axes: Interview Techniques, Personal Development, Team Working, Management, Matching Competencies, Leadership, Matching Strategy, Race & Diversity. Scale 0–10. Two dots marked as "Weaker Areas".

Identify your two lowest scoring skill areas. Rate these first and then the other skills areas, 1 (high priority) to 8 (low priority), and insert them in the activity chart below. Now identify activities that you will undertake to develop your skills in all areas. These activities will form the basis of your development plan.

Personal Action Planning

Activity Chart

Skill Area	Activity	Priority
Chapter 2 Personal Development		
Chapter 3 Team Working		
Chapter 4 Leadership		
Chapter 5 Management		

Personal Action Planning

Skill Area	Activity	Priority
Chapter 6 Matching to Core Competencies		
Chapter 7 Matching to Strategy		
Chapter 8 Race & Diversity		
Chapter 9 Interview Techniques		

Building a Development Plan

Now that you have a good idea of the areas in which you need to develop, the action planning chart can be used to help you write your development plan. There are two key issues that you will need to focus on:

- Writing Specific, Measurable, Achievable, Realistic and Timed (SMART) objectives that can be incorporated into the development plan. This plan can stand alone, specifically focused on the selection board, or it can be incorporated into your Performance Development Review (PDR)

- Identifying a work place coach and a mentor

You should share the spider graph and your activity plan with your line manager, personnel manager, coach or mentor to gain validation of your own assessment. In addition, they may be able to help you with ideas about actions that would improve your skills.

SMART Objectives

As a serving police officer you should be familiar with the writing of professional and development objectives for your PDR. What follows here is a review of the key principles that will enable you to refresh and refocus.

SMART is an acronym that can be used to help you write objectives. As a manager it can be a very effective tool for focusing team and individual objectives on your situational vision. In addition, as you will be aware, they can be used for managing performance or for developmental purposes.

There is considerable flexibility in the writing of objectives using the SMART approach as it can be used to provide emphasis and direction for individuals in the organisation. In particular, they can be used to make changes over the short, medium and long term. For example:

- **Short Term Operational Objectives**

    These can be directional and inform particular employees what is required and how they should do things. Operational strategies are often driven by this type of objective.

- **Medium Term Change Objectives**

    These are designed to change organisational culture and attitudes through gaining knowledge and changing behaviour. Objectives falling into this category are frequently used to address knowledge and behavioural change in areas like race and diversity.

- **Long Term Performance Objectives**

    This type of objective is often seen in long term force plans to indicate what will be achieved over a period of three or more years. They provide a focus for employees and they enable understanding of the intended direction of the force.

Action Words

It is most important that the objectives are dynamic and indicate what it is proposed to achieve. The words that are used are extremely important and should be strong action words (verbs). These words are easily understood and describe the type of action required to achieve the objective.

For example: to *plan*, to *write*, to *detect*, to *produce*, to *train*, to *select*, to *install* and to *investigate*. Each of these words creates the impression that an activity is to be undertaken to get something done. It is also very important to avoid words that are subjective and open to individual interpretation. The word to *know* is too broad but the word to *learn* is much more action focused and is measurable.

Motivational Objectives

It is important to inject an element of personal motivation when setting objectives. This enables you to be committed and focused on achieving the objective set. The more motivated you are the more likely you are to develop skills.

To initiate this motivational process the acronym SMART can become: **C - SMARTER**

The C stands for *Challenging*. The E stands for *Extending/Exciting* and the R stands for *Rewarding*.

By incorporating elements that fall into these catergories into the objective, you will motivate and energise employees. It can be argued that it does not matter what approach you use providing everyone in the organisation is pulling in the same direction. This is true, but a distinction should be drawn between business performance and personal development objectives.

SMART Definitions

(a) Specific

The definition of specific in this case means an objective that has an action, outcome or behaviour that can be measured by a quantity or percentage. If there is an objective to

Personal Action Planning

'respond quickly to immediate incidents', this is a description of an objective requiring a particular behaviour. However, there is no definition of 'quickly'. If the objective specified to 'respond within five minutes to immediate incidents', the objective can be measured. This wording makes the objective specific.

It follows that the wording is very important when producing a measurable objective. It can help to ask some questions when you are wording an objective. For example:

- **WHO** is to be involved?
- **WHAT** has to be done?
- **WHY** is this important?
- **WHERE** will these actions be completed?
- **WHEN** should it be completed?
- **HOW** will it be completed?

Specific objectives must be a description of an outcome that is measurable.

(b) Measurable

This means that whatever specific activity is undertaken there must be a process for measuring and recording performance.

In the case of the five minute target time to immediate incidents the response times must be measured and recorded to evaluate outcomes.

When setting any objective it must be measurable to provide a motivational force for successful completion.

Remember what gets measured gets done. So be careful!

Summary: Is there a reliable system in place to measure progress towards the achievement of the objective?

(c) Achievable

The objectives that are set must be capable of being achieved. There must be a likelihood success but that does not mean easy or simple.

The objectives need to be stretching and agreed by the parties involved.

Setting targets that are plainly ridiculous does not motivate people; it merely confirms their opinion of you as an idiot.

They will apply no energy or enthusiasm to a task that is futile.

Summary: With a reasonable amount of effort and application, can the objective be achieved?

(d) Relevant

This means two things: that the goal or target being set with the individual is something they can actually impact upon or change, and secondly, it is also important to the organisation.

Example: Telling the cleaners that they 'have to increase market share over the next financial quarter' is not actually something they can do anything about - it's not relevant to them. However, asking them to reduce expenditure on cleaning materials by £50 over the next three months is entirely relevant to them. It's what they spend their budget on every day. As to whether it's relevant to what the organisation is trying to achieve, the manager has to decide this by considering the wider picture.

Summary: Can the people with whom the objective is set make an impact on the situation? Do they have the necessary knowledge, authority and skill?

Commercial example:

SMART Objectives for ABC Ltd

- **Specific**: To obtain 5% market share within the first year of operations within our industry.

- **Measurable**: To sell 4000 units per month, which equates to approximately 5% market share.
- **Achievable**: Taking into account primary and secondary research and facts from our market share data, ABC Ltd do believe the objectives set are achievable.
- **Realistic**: Considering the amount of financial resources and manpower expertise we have at ABC Ltd, we believe the objectives set are realistic.
- **Time**: It is the expectation that the 5% market share objectives set for ABC Ltd will be achieved by the end of Dec 31st 2004.

Note: - there is no single correct way to write a SMART objective. It will depend on the nature of the objective and the intended use. The real test is to compare the statement against the SMART criteria you have chosen to use... does the statement tick all the boxes?

Coaching and Mentoring

It is important that you seek help in you development activities to create the best environment in which to learn and develop. A coach or a mentor is extremely useful and can be critical to your success. They can be of most benefit when you get into a new role, whether it is promotion or a specialist post.

Definitions

(a) Coaching is a process that enables an individual to learn and develop from a colleague in the work place to improve overall performance. A successful coach requires a detailed knowledge and understanding of the work place processes as well as the variety of styles, skills and techniques that are appropriate to the context in which the coaching takes place.

(b) Mentoring is assisting a person to make significant decisions or transitions in knowledge, work or thinking. Normally, the mentor will be an experienced individual but not necessarily fully aware of the work place context.

Contrasting coaching and mentoring

There are differences between coaching and mentoring. Coaching, particularly in its traditional sense, enables an individual to follow in the path of an older and wiser colleague who can pass on knowledge, experience and open doors to otherwise out-of-reach opportunities. Mentoring, on the other hand, is not generally performed on the basis that the mentor has direct experience of their subject's formal occupational role.

Finding a Coach and Mentor

Ideally, you seek out a coach and a mentor. There will be things you can discuss with one but not the other. This will give you greater flexibility to deal with issues that directly affect your development.

You should identify a coach in your work place that is experienced and fairly senior. This person will have a grasp of what the organisation stands for, the skills, attitudes and knowledge required to be successful. You will be able to learn from this individual through direct learning and get feedback on your performance.

A mentor outside the organisation is ideal. They will be experienced and senior and be able to share their experiences with you. This will enable you to broaden your perspectives on different issues and make the best possible decisions. Often a mentor can help you deal with difficult work place problems that you would not wish to raise with a coach.

What to expect of a coach or mentor

Coaching and mentoring share many similarities. They should operate to a set of principles. These are the principles that you can expect from an experienced coach or mentor.

Personal Action Planning

- Facilitate the exploration of needs, motivations, desires, skills and thought processes to assist the individual in making real, lasting change.
- Use questioning techniques to facilitate the subject's own thought processes in order to identify solutions and actions rather than take a wholly directive approach.
- Support the subject in setting appropriate goals and methods of assessing progress in relation to these goals.
- Observe, listen and ask questions to understand the subject's situation.
- Creatively apply tools and techniques which may include one-to-one training, facilitating, counselling and networking.
- Encourage a commitment to action and the development of lasting personal growth and change.
- Maintain unconditional positive regard for the subject, which means that the coach is at all times supportive and non-judgmental of the subject, their views, lifestyle and aspirations.
- Ensure that the subject develops personal competencies, and does not develop unhealthy dependencies on the coaching or mentoring relationship.
- Evaluate the outcomes of the process, using objective measures wherever possible to ensure the relationship is

successful and the subject is achieving their personal goals.
- Encourage subjects to continually improve competencies, and to develop new developmental alliances where necessary to achieve their goals.
- Work within their area of personal competence.
- Possess qualifications and experience in the areas that skills-transfer coaching is offered.
- Manage the relationship to ensure the subject receives the appropriate level of service and that programmes are neither too short, nor too long.

Experiential Learning

If you have made it this far you will have a number of ideas as to how you will take your development programme forward. Whatever that might look like, there is one principle that you should understand and acknowledge: there is no substitute for experience. No matter how much you read about the topics in this book or how long you muse over the theoretical basis for each of them, there comes a time when the only way to learn is to do it. Whatever your learning style looks like, all of the topics discussed in this book require practical delivery. You will never lead people purely because you have read a book about it; you must interact with people and use your behaviours to impact on the people

Personal Action Planning

involved. Only then will you discover whether your behaviour is effective or not. If it is not you will need to readjust your approach and see if the change has the required outcome. If not do it again.

This is practical *experiential learning*. Only through having the experience will you learn from the outcomes. Also, you will be able to take into account your learning style and adapt the practical experience to meet your particular needs. This means your learning will be 'active' and have positive outcomes.

The outcomes of this approach will be:

- lessons learned will be relevant to you
- you will develop a sense of personal responsibility for your own learning

Experiential learning has many benefits for individuals:

- increased long term retention
- increased interest in learning
- meeting the needs of different learning styles
- expanding the experience we already possess

These benefits further stress the importance of learning through experience. Perhaps the following statement precisely identifies the need for experiential learning:

"Learning is not a spectator sport. Learners do not learn much by just sitting and listening, memorising pre-packaged assignments and spitting out answers. They must talk about what they are learning, write about it, relate it to past experiences, and apply it to their daily lives. They must make what they learn part of themselves."

A.W. Chickering and Z.F. Gamson
'Seven Principles for Good Practice'

The underlying premise of this approach is that you should be motivated to learn when there is a *need to know* or do something in order *to perform more effectively.*

The Experiential Learning Model

Step 1 – Knowledge

The first step is to gain and understand the theoretical basis to the concepts and skills being presented and to focus on the Knowledge, Skills or Attitudes (KSA) being considered.

Step 2 - Experiencing

In this phase you should be involved in a practical exercise, working in a safe environment, where the KSA being studied are practiced. The purpose is to provide you with a practical experience of using the theoretical concepts and understand their relevancy.

Step 3 – Reflecting

After the exercise you should reflect on the structured activity. The purpose is to critically analyse the activity and relate them to similar past experiences.

Step 4 – Thinking

At this stage you should think about the lessons coming out of the theory and practical exercises to build on knowledge or to create new knowledge.

Step 5 – Modifying

After thinking you can use the information to critically assess what you currently do and modify how you do it in the future in the light of what has been learned.

Step 6 – Active Experimentation

This is the stage where you practice what has been learned by incorporating the knowledge, skills or attitudes into daily work life.

Personal Action Planning

Step 7 – Integrating

This requires a review of the learning within a fixed time frame. The key questions are:

"To what extent have I <u>learned</u> the new information, skills or attitudes?"

"To what extent have I <u>used</u> the new knowledge, skills or attitudes in the performance of my real life roles?"

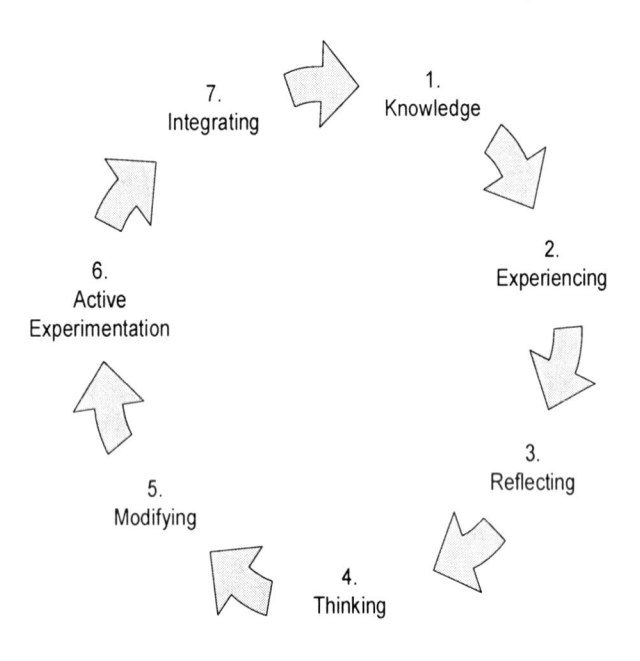

1. Knowledge
2. Experiencing
3. Reflecting
4. Thinking
5. Modifying
6. Active Experimentation
7. Integrating

Personal Action Planning

I hope that you will enjoy this approach to personal development and find it inspiring.

Appendices

1. National Occupational Standards

2. About ISP Consultancy Ltd.

Appendix 1

National Occupational Standards
(Source: Skills for Justice 2007)

Unit Title

AA1 - Promote equality and value diversity

Summary

This unit is about promoting equality and valuing the diversity of people. This is an essential aspect of all jobs in the justice sector and is appropriate to people working at all levels and in all posts. It should form the basis of everything that any worker in the sector does.

The term 'people' is used broadly to cover any child, adult, group, community or agency that workers come into contact with, either directly or indirectly. It includes members of the public, individuals who are clients of the justice sector, and colleagues in the workplace.

There is one element:

AA1.1 - Promote equality and value diversity

National Occupational Standards

Target Group

The unit is designed to be applicable to everyone who works in the justice sector at every level of work.

Linked Units

This unit is designed to underpin all other units as promoting equality and valuing diversity is an essential component of all actions in the sector.

Place in Qualifications

It is proposed that this unit should be an integral part of all qualifications in the justice sector.

Performance Criteria

To meet the standard, you:

1. act in accordance with legislation, employment regulations and policies, and codes of practice related to promoting equality and valuing diversity
2. act in ways that:

- acknowledge and recognise individuals' background and beliefs
- respect diversity
- value people as individuals
- do not discriminate against people

3. provide individuals with the information they need to make informed decisions about exercising their rights
4. provide information in a format appropriate to the individual
5. take account of how your behaviour affects individuals and their experience of your organisation's culture and approach
6. seek feedback from individuals on your behaviour and use this to improve what you do in the future
7. challenge people when they are not promoting equality and valuing diversity
8. actively help others to promote equality and value diversity
9. seek support from appropriate sources when you are having difficulty understanding how to promote equality and value diversity.

Range

Help others by:
(a) supporting them when they are promoting equality and valuing diversity
(b) sharing information about how to promote equality and value diversity.

Explanatory Notes

In performance criteria 1 and 2 'act' might relate to direct or indirect interactions with people.

In performance criterion 1. Legislation, employment regulations and policies, and codes of practice will include:
- age
- employment
- dependents (people who have caring responsibilities and those who do not)
- disability
- gender and transgender
- human rights (including those of children)
- language
- learning disabilities
- marital status / civil partnership
- mental health / illness
- political opinion
- racial group
- religious belief and non-belief
- sexual orientation
- Welsh language.

In performance criterion 2, this would include:
- how you interact with people
- when you interact
- why you interact
- what is the nature of the interaction
- what information you record and how you record it.

In performance criterion 9, an appropriate source for support might be:
- colleagues

- external agencies, associations and groups with a focus on equality and diversity
- learning and development opportunities
- line manager
- specific support services arranged within the organisation
- staff association / trade union
- written / electronic materials.

Knowledge and Understanding

To meet the standard, you need to know and understand:
1. the legislation, employment regulations and policies, and codes of practice that apply to the promotion of equality and diversity and how you need to apply these
2. the benefits of diversity and the promotion of equality
3. the wide variety of forms that discrimination may take and how these manifest themselves
4. how inequality and discrimination affects individuals, groups and communities and society as a whole
5. why the promotion of equality and valuing of diversity is of vital importance if you are to work effectively in the justice sector
6. what the promotion of equality and valuing of diversity means for you in your day-to-day work

7. how you can promote equality and diversity whilst protecting people from the risk of harm
8. your own areas for personal growth in to promoting equality and valuing diversity and how this will benefit you as an individual
9. the effect of cultural differences on verbal and non-verbal communication
10. how to behave and communicate in ways that:
    a. support equality and diversity
    b. do not exclude or offend people
    c. challenge discrimination effectively
    d. respect individuals' differences
    e. do not abuse the status and power that you have
    f. recognise the difficulties in communication and language in your area of work
11. how your behaviour contributes to your organisation's culture and your responsibility for developing a positive culture for all
12. how joint working with other agencies and workers can help in the promotion of diversity
13. how to provide the information that individuals are entitled to receive and ensure it is clear and helpful
14. the actions (yours and other's) that undermine equality and diversity and

what to do about this (including when these people are senior to you)
15. what to do about systems and structures when they do not promote equality and value diversity
16. the actions you can take to help other people promote equality and value diversity and how to do this effectively
17. the actions you can take to value the people you are interacting with and enable them to interact with you
18. why you should seek support when you are having difficulty promoting equality and valuing diversity, where this support can be gained and how to use it effectively.

For NVQ/SVQ assessment

Assessment Guidance

When planning assessment, candidates should consider how they may best use evidence across a number of units. By its nature practice against this standard should be evident in everything that individuals do at work. Candidates and assessors should think about how they can use evidence from their day-to-day work activities towards achievement of this unit.

Candidates may wish to use these **sources of evidence:**

1. products of their work
2. notes and drafts of their analysis during the process of producing those products
3. evidence from others who worked with the candidate
4. records and correspondence
5. their reflective practice journal.

In order to demonstrate competence the candidate must be able to show consistent competent performance.

In this unit evidence from performance is required and should be the primary source of evidence, but this will often be supported by questioning or other forms in order to gather evidence of the candidate's ability to perform competently across all the range items listed.

Evidence requirements

Evidence from performance

The candidate's package of evidence from their performance should be drawn from real working practices and needs to cover all the performance criteria and all of the aspects of **range.**

Simulations cannot be used to provide evidence for this unit except for performance criterion 8 and range 1 where professional discussion, candidate reports and / or simulation might be used.

Evidence from knowledge and understanding

Candidates must provide evidence of their knowledge and understanding in the areas detailed in the knowledge and understanding section of the standard. Much of their knowledge and understanding will be evident in how they plan, carry out and review their work, and the critical decision-making inherent in this process. Where the candidate's knowledge and understanding is not evident from their performance, it may be necessary for additional evidence of knowledge and understanding to be provided.

Unit Title

AA2 - Develop a culture and systems that promote equality and value diversity

Summary

This unit is about developing a culture and systems within an organisation to promote equality and value diversity i.e. setting the context in which others in an organisation are themselves able to promote equality and value diversity.

There is one element

AA2.1 Develop a culture and systems that promote equality and value diversity

Target Group

The unit is for managers in organisations who have a functional senior responsibility and accountability for developing a culture and systems that promote equality and value diversity within their part of the organisation.

Linked units

This unit is a key requirement for senior managers in the justice sector as the promotion of equality and valuing of diversity is an essential component of all actions in the sector.

Element

AA2.1 Develop a culture and systems that promote equality and value diversity

Performance criteria

To meet the standard, you

1. interpret relevant legislation and employment regulations to inform how equality and individuals' rights and responsibilities should be promoted, and diversity valued, in your organisation

National Occupational Standards

2. evaluate the effectiveness of your organisation's systems, policies, procedures and guidelines in promoting equality and valuing diversity

3. take the appropriate actions to ensure that your organisation's systems, policies, procedures and guidelines do promote equality and value diversity

4. actively promote equality and value diversity

5. actively demonstrate by your behaviour the promotion of equality and valuing of diversity

6. regularly review your organisation's systems and processes and improve them to address issues related to unfair and discriminatory practice

7. actively support individuals whose rights have been compromised in having their complaints appropriately addressed

8. actively challenge the discriminatory behaviour of individuals and institutional discrimination.

Range

1. Evaluate

National Occupational Standards

- a) formal (e.g. equality impact assessments)
- b) informal.

2. Actively promote and value by:

    - a) profiling the workforce and promoting a diverse workforce

    - b) acting as a mentor / role model for people in relation to equality and diversity

    - c) involving diverse groups in different pieces of work

    - d) setting objectives for own team to promote equality and value diversity

    - e) ensuring that the organisational processes that you are responsible for are fair (e.g. recruitment and selection)

    - f) regularly seeking the views of under represented groups on their experiences (in the organisation and the local population) and acting on them

    - g) communicating the importance of equality and diversity at every opportunity linking it to the wider work of the organisation.

Explanatory notes

In performance criterion 1. Legislation and employment regulations relate to:

- age

- employment

- dependents – people who have caring responsibilities and those who do not

- disability

- gender and transgender

- human rights (including those of children)

- language

- learning disabilities

- marital status / civil partnership

- mental health / illness
- political opinion

- racial group

- religious belief and non-belief

- sexual orientation

- Welsh language.

In performance criteria 2 and 3, organisation's systems, policies, procedures and guidelines will include those relating to:

- the management and development of people in your organisation (i.e. recruitment, selection, management, appraisal, training and development, disciplinary etc)

- the services offered by your organisation to the public

- the views of staff (e.g. through staff surveys)

1. complaints processes
2. grievance procedures.

Knowledge and understanding for unit AA2

To meet the standard, you need to know and understand:

1. how to interpret current and emerging relevant legislation and employment regulations that apply to the promotion of equality and the valuing of diversity

2. your duty of care under legislation and employment regulations

3. the benefits of diversity and the promotion of equality

4. how inequality and discrimination affect individuals, groups and communities and society as a whole

5. why the promotion of equality and valuing of diversity is of vital importance in the justice sector

6. how the promotion of equality and valuing of diversity can be actively promoted by you in your day-to-day work and in a way which inspires others to see its value

7. the meaning of the term 'organisational culture', who this is set by and your role in this

8. the affect of organisational culture on groups who are a minority in the workforce and how they may respond as a result

9. how the promotion of equality and valuing of diversity can be built into the culture and systems of your organisation and the reasons for doing this

National Occupational Standards

10. how leadership roles and styles can be used in the promotion of equality and diversity and in challenging individual discrimination and institutional discrimination

11. how you can use complaints and grievance processes as a way of tackling discrimination and oppression

12. your own areas for personal growth in relation to promoting equality and valuing diversity and how this will benefit you as an individual

13. how the promotion of equality and valuing of diversity may be affected by systems and structures and your role in actively tackling these

14. the actions you may need to take to help other people promote equality and value diversity and how to do this effectively

15. what you need to do to support people whose rights have been compromised (including ensuring that adequate support systems are in place)

16. how you can actively challenge individual and organisational discrimination, the risks that you might be taking in doing

National Occupational Standards

this and why it is necessary to take these risks

17. who can support you in challenging individual and organisational discrimination

18. effective methods of evaluating the effectiveness of equality and diversity policies and procedures

19. how you can contribute to developing and implementing good and best practice in relation to equality and diversity

20. why you should seek support when you are having difficulty understanding how to promote equality and diversity, where this support can be gained and how to use it effectively.

(Source: Skills for Justice)

Appendix 2

About ISP Consultancy

Introduction

ISP Consultancy was established by Ian Hutchison following a career with Thames Valley Police.

After military service in the mid 1970s he joined the police service and pursued an exciting and challenging career during which he was promoted though the ranks to Chief Superintendent.

He served at various places across the Thames Valley gaining wide policing experience including working in urban and rural areas, managing major police operations, working on national policing projects and leading the Serious Crime Squad in surveillance and investigation of major crime.

He is a law graduate, has masters in criminology, a Fellow of the Chartered Management Institute and a member of the British Psychological Society.

ISP Consultancy

ISP Consultancy is a highly professional and experienced training organisation that specialises in assisting people to join the police service and pursue successful careers.

ISP is the only company in the U.K. that offers comprehensive training packages for potential police recruits and serving officers. It provides assistance in the preliminary stages when you are considering a police career, takes you through the police national selection process and, after appointment as a constable or sergeant, assists you with career progression.

Courses and Services

Police Recruits

Joining the police service is one of the most important life decisions you will make. It is essential you get it right. To assist you we provide:

- aptitude testing for police work
- assistance with the application process
- half-day seminars
- one-to-one coaching
- interview techniques courses

Courses and seminars are run at locations across the country.

About ISP Consultancy

All of our graduates pass Stage 1 (Application) and Stage 2 (Assessment Centre). We are proud of our high pass rate. We routinely achieve some of the highest pass marks in the country – 72%, 74%, 75%, 76%, 78% and 80%!

Application Form

The Application Form is the first stage in the selection process. It requires you to provide a considerable amount of personal information to enable the police to determine whether you fit the recruitment criteria. In addition, the application form contains 9 questions that you will have to answer. The first 4 questions are 'Competency Based Questions' (CBQ) that require you to provide answers demonstrating you have the basic life experiences and skills to enable your progression to the Assessment Centre stage.

After submitting the application the answers are marked and graded 'A', 'B', 'C' or 'D'. To pass the application stage you will have to attain a grade 'B', or higher, overall. If you fail this first stage of the process you will have to wait 6 months before you can reapply.

It goes without saying that you must take the greatest care in completing the application form and, in particular, formulating your answers to the 4 competency based questions.

Many people fail at this stage because they do not understand what is required.

ISP will assist you to understand what is required and advise you accordingly. We do not fill in the application for you, tell you what to write or what phrases and words to use. If we did that it would be unethical and you would be submitting an application, which is not yours! However, we will help you understand the general principles and how to discover suitable life experiences that will evidence the competencies required.

All of our applicants that take advantage of this assistance go through to the assessment stage.

We also pride ourselves in striking a personal relationship with our clients. You are not just a client; you will become a friend of ISP and we will act as your mentor and source of guidance as your career progresses.

Development Seminars an One-to-One

Prior to every national assessment session we run a series of half day seminars and one-to-one coaching.

The seminars are a great way of learning and practising skills with a small group of other candidates. You will learn from each other and gain the confidence to know you can achieve

About ISP Consultancy

well beyond the standard required. If you are unable to attend the seminars or you need more development work, one-to-one sessions will be available to you.

The Police Selection Development Seminars (PSDS) have two objectives.

- To explain the challenge of the police selection assessment centre.
- To provide you with a 'tool kit' that you can use to develop your skills over the period leading up to your assessment.

The course will provide everything you need to know about the process. You will learn how to match yourself to the core competencies and how to approach the individual exercises.

You will understand and practice, in a safe environment, the verbal logical reasoning test, numerical reasoning test, interactive scenarios, written exercises and competency based interview. You should not feel apprehensive about any of this because it is designed to be fun!

We know from experience that the secret to success is more than just understanding what is required; it is in your ability to 'demonstrate' the skills.

About ISP Consultancy

You will also receive a comprehensive Study Pack that you will take away with you to reinforce your learning.

The course enables you to network with other applicants and ISP will support you through the process with advice and guidance.

We will be honest with you about your areas of strength and areas where development is required. As a result you will be clear where you need to focus your development plan.

Our experience is that the course lives up to the two stated objectives and delegates quickly become aware of what development they need to reach the standard required.

The seminars normally run six weeks prior to each of the Assessment Centre on Saturday mornings from 9 am until 1 pm and weekdays.

'The Police Selection Process' by Ian Hutchison ISBN 0-9554307-0-4

This book is a practical guide to the selection process for all who are aspiring to a police career as a constable, community support officer or special constable.

The book provides an explanation of the process and techniques for dealing with all the exercises. It includes:

- Application form
- Assessment centre
- Core competencies
- Competency based interview
- Interactive scenarios
- Written exercises
- Numerical test
- Verbal logical reasoning test
- Entry criteria
- Frequently asked questions

There are also practice tests for the numerical, verbal logical reasoning test and the written exercises.

In addition, there is a chapter on interview technique for those candidates that are applying to forces that require candidates to undergo a filter interview before or after the assessment centre.

Demonstration DVD

To complement the skills learned on the Police Selection Development Seminars and the paperback book there is a demonstration DVD is available. Two potential police recruits illustrate what will be required of you at the Assessment Centre in the Interactive Scenarios and the Competency Based Interview. This is essential viewing for all potential recruits to enable you to understand and assimilate the seven point plan and the structured interview.

The DVD can be purchased through the web site www.ispconsultancy.com.

Serving Officers

Specialist roles, promotion and High Potential Development Scheme

After you are appointed as a serving police officer we will assist you with your career development so that you can get into a specialist role, pass promotion selection boards or get you on the High Potential Development Scheme.

ISP works with police forces across the country helping officers with personal development, team working and leadership. We operate inside and outside the police service so we are aware of developments in policing and the impact on police officers.

Interview Techniques

The police service is always seeking to identify the most highly motivated and skilled people to fill promotion vacancies, specialist posts and place future leaders on the High Potential Development Scheme (HPDS). In each case most selection processes incorporate some form of presentation or assessment centre.

The common feature, in nearly all cases, is the

About ISP Consultancy

Police Selection Board.

At some point you will have to sit in front of a panel, answer questions and tell them about yourself. This is the hardest step for most people, is often intimidating and can feel as if the whole process is shrouded in mystery.

ISP Interview Techniques training is designed to demystify the board process and prepare you for the challenge. The training is delivered as a single day course or as a package tailored for individuals and explains how you should prepare for the big day and how to deal with the practical aspects of the interview. You will learn the fundamentals of:

- Team working
- Principles of effective management
- Discovering your personality
- Matching personality to role & strategy
- Setting the agenda for the interview
- Dealing with topics
- Answering questions
- Structuring your preparation
- Developing leadership behaviours
- Managing the practicalities of the interview

The courses have a balanced number of delegates to allow you to maximise your learning in the time available. Overall, the training is relaxed, fun and designed so you can prepare yourself for the selection interview.

In addition, you will receive a comprehensive Study Pack and be supported with advice and guidance.

All of this adds up to an unforgettable learning experience. These skills only need to be learned once. You will reap the benefits throughout your career. For more information take a look at our web site:
www.ispconsultancy.co.uk

Lightning Source UK Ltd.
Milton Keynes UK
01 October 2009

144401UK00001B/1/P

9 780955 430718